MznLnx

Missing Links Exam Preps

Exam Prep for

Mathematical Ideas

Miller et al..., 10th Edition

The MznLnx Exam Prep is your link from the texbook and lecture to your exams.
The MznLnx Exam Preps are unauthorized and comprehensive reviews of your textbooks.

All material provided by MznLnx and Rico Publications (c) 2010
Textbook publishers and textbook authors do not particpate in or contribute to these reviews.

MznLnx

Rico
Publications

Exam Prep for Mathematical Ideas
10th Edition
Miller et al...

Publisher: Raymond Houge
Assistant Editor: Michael Rouger
Text and Cover Designer: Lisa Buckner
Marketing Manager: Sara Swagger
Project Manager, Editorial Production: Jerry Emerson
Art Director: Vernon Lowerui

Product Manager: Dave Mason
Editorial Asitant: Rachel Guzmanji
Pedagogy: Debra Long
Cover Image: Jim Reed/Getty Images
Text and Cover Printer: City Printing, Inc.
Compositor: Media Mix, Inc.

(c) 2010 Rico Publications
ALL RIGHTS RESERVED. No part of this work
covered by the copyright may be reproduced or
used in any form or by an means--graphic, electronic,
or mechanical, including photocopying, recording,
taping, Web distribution, information storage, and
retrieval systems, or in any other manner--without the
written permission of the publisher.

Printed in the United States
ISBN:

For more information about our products, contact us at:
Dave.Mason@RicoPublications.com

For permission to use material from this text or
product, submit a request online to:
Dave.Mason@RicoPublications.com

Contents

CHAPTER 1
The Art of Problem Solving — 1

CHAPTER 2
The Basic Concepts of Set Theory — 11

CHAPTER 3
Introduction to Logic — 21

CHAPTER 4
Numeration and Mathematical Systems — 26

CHAPTER 5
Number Theory — 36

CHAPTER 6
The Real Numbers and Their Representations — 50

CHAPTER 7
The Basic Concepts of Algebra — 63

CHAPTER 8
Graphs, Functions, and Systems of Equations and Inequalities — 77

CHAPTER 9
Geometry — 92

CHAPTER 10
Trigonometry — 114

CHAPTER 11
Counting Methods — 123

CHAPTER 12
Probability — 128

CHAPTER 13
Statistics — 136

CHAPTER 14
Consumer Mathematics — 150

ANSWER KEY — 159

TO THE STUDENT

COMPREHENSIVE

The *MznLnx* Exam Prep series is designed to help you pass your exams. Editors at MznLnx review your textbooks and then prepare these practice exams to help you master the textbook material. Unlike study guides, workbooks, and practice tests provided by the texbook publisher and textbook authors, *MznLnx* gives you **all** of the material in each chapter in exam form, not just samples, so you can be sure to nail your exam.

MECHANICAL

The MznLnx Exam Prep series creates exams that will help you learn the subject matter as well as test you on your understanding. Each question is designed to help you master the concept. Just working through the exams, you gain an understanding of the subject--its a simple mechanical process that produces success.

INTEGRATED STUDY GUIDE AND REVIEW

MznLnx is not just a set of exams designed to test you, its also a comprehensive review of the subject content. Each exam question is also a review of the concept, making sure that you will get the answer correct without having to go to other sources of material. You learn as you go! Its the easiest way to pass an exam.

HUMOR

Studying can be tedious and dry. MznLnx's instructional design includes moderate humor within the exam questions on occassion, to break the tedium and revitalize the brain

Chapter 1. The Art of Problem Solving

1. _____ is a general term for any type of information processing. This includes phenomena ranging from human thinking to calculations with a more narrow meaning. _____ is a process following a well-defined model that is understood and can be expressed in an algorithm, protocol, network topology, etc.
   a. 2-3 heap
   b. 120-cell
   c. Computation
   d. 1-center problem

2. _____ refers to any mathematics of the peoples of Mesopotamia, from the days of the early Sumerians to the fall of Babylon in 539 BC. In contrast to the scarcity of sources in Egyptian mathematics, our knowledge of _____ is derived from some 400 clay tablets unearthed since the 1850s. Written in Cuneiform script, tablets were inscribed while the clay was moist, and baked hard in an oven or by the heat of the sun.
   a. 1-center problem
   b. Babylonian mathematics
   c. 2-3 heap
   d. 120-cell

3. In mathematics, a _____ can mean either an element of the set {1, 2, 3, ...} or an element of the set {0, 1, 2, 3, ...}. The latter is especially preferred in mathematical logic, set theory, and computer science.

   _____s have two main purposes: they can be used for counting, and they can be used for ordering.

   a. Cardinal numbers
   b. Natural number
   c. Strong partition cardinal
   d. Suslin cardinal

4. _____, as that term is used in this article, is the mathematics written in Greek, developed from the 6th century BC to the 5th century AD around the Eastern shores of the Mediterranean. The word 'mathematics' itself derives from the ancient Greek μαθημα, meaning 'subject of instruction'.. The study of mathematics for its own sake and the use of generalized mathematical theories and proofs is the key difference between _____ and those of preceding civilizations.
   a. 1-center problem
   b. 120-cell
   c. 2-3 heap
   d. Greek mathematics

5. Induction or _____, sometimes called inductive logic, is the process of reasoning in which the premises of an argument are believed to support the conclusion but do not entail it;. Induction is a form of reasoning that makes generalizations based on individual instances. It is used to ascribe properties or relations to types based on an observation instance; or to formulate laws based on limited observations of recurring phenomenal patterns.
   a. Affine logic
   b. Inductive reasoning
   c. Idempotency of entailment
   d. Intuitionistic logic

6. A _____ is a building where the upper surfaces are triangular and converge on one point. The base of _____s are usually quadrilateral or trilateral, meaning that a _____ usually has four or five faces. A _____'s design, with the majority of the weight closer to the ground, means that less material higher up on the _____ will be pushing down from above.
   a. 1-center problem
   b. 120-cell
   c. Pyramid
   d. 2-3 heap

7. In mathematics, hyperbolic n-space, denoted H^n, is the maximally symmetric, simply connected, n-dimensional Riemannian manifold with constant sectional curvature −1. _____ is the principal example of a space exhibiting hyperbolic geometry. It can be thought of as the negative-curvature analogue of the n-sphere.

Chapter 1. The Art of Problem Solving

    a. Horocycle
    b. Hyperbolic space
    c. Hyperbolic geometry
    d. Margulis lemma

8. _____ is the title of a short book on logic by Gottlob Frege, published in 1879, and is also the name of the formal system set out in that book.

_____ is usually translated as concept writing or concept notation; the full title of the book identifies it as 'a formula language, modelled on that of arithmetic, of pure thought.' The _____ was arguably the most important publication in logic since Aristotle founded the subject. Frege's motivation for developing his formal approach to logic resembled Leibniz's motivation for his calculus ratiocinator.

    a. 2-3 heap
    b. 1-center problem
    c. Begriffsschrift
    d. 120-cell

9. In mathematics, the _____ or Pythagoras' theorem is a relation in Euclidean geometry among the three sides of a right triangle. The theorem is named after the Greek mathematician Pythagoras, who by tradition is credited with its discovery and proof, although it is often argued that knowledge of the theory predates him.. The theorem is as follows:

In any right triangle, the area of the square whose side is the hypotenuse is equal to the sum of the areas of the squares whose sides are the two legs.

    a. 120-cell
    b. 2-3 heap
    c. 1-center problem
    d. Pythagorean theorem

10. A _____ is a software program that facilitates symbolic mathematics. The core functionality of a CAS is manipulation of mathematical expressions in symbolic form.

Chapter 1. The Art of Problem Solving

The symbolic manipulations supported typically include

- simplification to the smallest possible expression or some standard form, including automatic simplification with assumptions and simplification with constraints
- substitution of symbolic, functors or numeric values for expressions
- change of form of expressions: expanding products and powers, partial and full factorization, rewriting as partial fractions, constraint satisfaction, rewriting trigonometric functions as exponentials, etc.
- partial and total differentiation
- symbolic constrained and unconstrained global optimization
- solution of linear and some non-linear equations over various domains
- solution of some differential and difference equations
- taking some limits
- some indefinite and definite integration, including multidimensional integrals
- integral transforms
- arbitrary-precision numeric operations
- Series operations such as expansion, summation and products
- matrix operations including products, inverses, etc.
- display of mathematical expressions in two-dimensional mathematical form, often using typesetting systems similar to TeX
- add-ons for use in applied mathematics such as physics packages for physical computation
- plotting graphs and parametric plots of functions in two and three dimensions, and animating them
- APIs for linking it on an external program such as a database, or using in a programming language to use the _____
- drawing charts and diagrams
- string manipulation such as matching and searching
- statistical computation
- Theorem proving and verification
- graphic production and editing such as CGI and signal processing as image processing
- sound synthesis

Many also include a programming language, allowing users to implement their own algorithms.

Some _____s focus on a specific area of application; these are typically developed in academia and are free.

a. 1-center problem
b. 2-3 heap
c. 120-cell
d. Computer algebra system

11. A _____ is a 2D geometric symbolic representation of information according to some visualization technique. Sometimes, the technique uses a 3D visualization which is then projected onto the 2D surface. The word graph is sometimes used as a synonym for _____.

a. 1-center problem
b. 120-cell
c. 2-3 heap
d. Diagram

Chapter 1. The Art of Problem Solving

12. In mathematics, a _____ is a statement that can be proved on the basis of explicitly stated or previously agreed assumptions.
    a. Logical value
    b. Disjunction introduction
    c. Theorem
    d. Boolean function

13. A _____ is a simple shape of Euclidean geometry consisting of those points in a plane which are at a constant distance, called the radius, from a fixed point, called the center. A _____ with center A is sometimes denoted by the symbol A.

    A chord of a _____ is a line segment whose two endpoints lie on the _____.

    a. Malfatti circles
    b. Circular segment
    c. Circumcircle
    d. Circle

14. _____ is the likelihood or chance that something is the case or will happen. Theoretical _____ is used extensively in areas such as statistics, mathematics, science and philosophy to draw conclusions about the likelihood of potential events and the underlying mechanics of complex systems.

    The word _____ does not have a consistent direct definition.

    a. Discrete random variable
    b. Probability
    c. Statistical significance
    d. Standardized moment

15. _____ Galilei (15 February 1564 - 8 January 1642) was a Tuscan physicist, mathematician, astronomer, and philosopher who played a major role in the Scientific Revolution. His achievements include improvements to the telescope and consequent astronomical observations, and support for Copernicanism. _____ has been called the 'father of modern observational astronomy', the 'father of modern physics', the 'father of science', and 'the Father of Modern Science.' The motion of uniformly accelerated objects, taught in nearly all high school and introductory college physics courses, was studied by _____ as the subject of kinematics.
    a. David Naccache
    b. Francesco Severi
    c. Jan Kowalewski
    d. Galileo

16. In mathematics, an arithmetic progression or _____ is a sequence of numbers such that the difference of any two successive members of the sequence is a constant. For instance, the sequence 3, 5, 7, 9, 11, 13... is an arithmetic progression with common difference 2.
    a. Edgeworth series
    b. Alternating series test
    c. Eisenstein series
    d. Arithmetic sequence

17. Leonardo of Pisa (c. 1170 - c. 1250), also known as Leonardo Pisano, Leonardo Bonacci, Leonardo _____, or, most commonly, simply _____, was an Italian mathematician, considered by some 'the most talented mathematician of the Middle Ages'.
    a. Ralph C. Merkle
    b. Harry Hinsley
    c. Guido Castelnuovo
    d. Fibonacci

18. A _____, from the French patron, is a type of theme of recurring events of or objects, sometimes referred to as elements of a set. These elements repeat in a predictable manner. It can be a template or model which can be used to generate things or parts of a thing, especially if the things that are created have enough in common for the underlying _____ to be inferred, in which case the things are said to exhibit the unique _____.

    a. 2-3 heap
    b. 120-cell
    c. 1-center problem
    d. Pattern

19. A _____ is a number that can be represented as a regular and discrete geometric pattern. If the pattern is polytopic, the figurate is labeled a polytopic number, and may be a polygonal number or a polyhedral number.

The first few triangular numbers can be built from rows of 1, 2, 3, 4, 5, and 6 items:

The n-th regular r-topic number is given by the formula:

$$P_r(n) = \binom{n+r-1}{r} = \frac{n^{(r)}}{r!} \quad \text{for } n \geq 1$$

r! is the factorial of r, $\binom{n}{r}$ is a binomial coefficient, and n is the rising factorial.

    a. Heptagonal number
    b. Centered pentagonal number
    c. Square number
    d. Figurate number

20. A _____ is a figurate number that extends the concept of triangular and square numbers to the pentagon, but, unlike the first two, the patterns involved in the construction of _____s are not rotationally symmetrical. The nth _____ p_n is the number of distinct dots in a pattern of dots consisting of the outlines of regular pentagons whose sides contain 1 to n dots, overlaid so that they share one vertex. For instance, the third one is formed from outlines comprising 1, 5 and 10 dots, but the 1, and 3 of the 5, coincide with 3 of the 10 - leaving 12 distinct dots, 10 in the form of a pentagon, and 2 inside...

    a. Pentagonal number
    b. Critical line theorem
    c. Multiplicative partition
    d. Holonomic constant

21. A _____ is the sum of the n natural numbers from 1 to n.

$$T_n = 1 + 2 + 3 + \cdots + (n-1) + n = \frac{n(n+1)}{2} = \frac{n^2+n}{2} \overset{\text{def}}{=} \binom{n+1}{2}$$

As shown in the rightmost term of this formula, every _____ is a binomial coefficient: the nth triangular is the number of distinct pairs to be selected from n + 1 objects. In this form it solves the 'handshake problem' of counting the number of handshakes if each person in a room full of n+1 total people shakes hands once with each other person.

    a. Triangular number
    b. Star number
    c. Centered pentagonal number
    d. Heptagonal number

22. The _____ program is a directory search utility on Unix-like platforms. It searches through one or more directory trees of a filesystem, locating files based on some user-specified criteria. By default, _____ returns all files below the current working directory.
   a. 120-cell
   b. 2-3 heap
   c. 1-center problem
   d. Find

23. In mathematics, a _____ for a given base is a non-negative integer, the representation of whose square in that base can be split into two parts that add up to the original number again. For example, 297 is a _____ for base 10, because $297^2 = 88209$, which can be split into 88 and 209, and 88 + 209 = 297. The second part may start with the digit 0, but must be positive.
   a. Truncatable prime
   b. Smith number
   c. Sum-product number
   d. Kaprekar number

24. A _____ is a figurate number that represents a heptagon. The n-th _____ is given by the formula

$$\frac{5n^2 - 3n}{2}.$$

The first few _____s are:

1, 7, 18, 34, 55, 81, 112, 148, 189, 235, 286, 342, 403, 469, 540, 616, 697, 783, 874, 970

The parity of _____s follows the pattern odd-odd-even-even.

   a. Hexagonal number
   b. Pentagonal pyramidal number
   c. Star number
   d. Heptagonal number

25. A _____ is a figurate number, The nth _____ will be the number of points in a hexagon with n regularly spaced points on a side, as shown in .

The formula for the nth _____

$$h_n = n(2n - 1)$$

The first few _____s are:

1, 6, 15, 28, 45, 66, 91, 120, 153, 190, 231, 276, 325, 378, 435, 496, 561, 630, 703, 780, 861, 946

Every _____ is a triangular number, but not every triangular number is a _____. Like a triangular number, the digital root in base 10 of a _____ can only be 1, 3, 6, or 9.

   a. Centered pentagonal number
   b. Tetrahedral number
   c. Hexagonal number
   d. Polygonal number

26. An _____ is a figurate number that represents an octagon. The _____ for n is given by the formula 3n² - 2n, with n > 0. The first few _____s are:

1, 8, 21, 40, 65, 96, 133, 176, 225, 280, 341, 408, 481, 560, 645, 736, 833, 936

_____s can be formed by placing triangular numbers on the four sides of a square.

   a. A chemical equation
   b. A Mathematical Theory of Communication
   c. Octahedral number
   d. Octagonal number

27. A _____ or enneagonal number is a figurate number that represents a nonagon. The _____ for n is given by the formula:

$$\frac{7n^2 - 5n}{2}.$$

The first few _____s are:

   1, 9, 24, 46, 75, 111, 154, 204, 261, 325, 396, 474, 559, 651, 750, 856, 969, 1089, 1216, 1350, 1491, 1639, 1794, 1956, 2125, 2301, 2484, 2674, 2871, 3075, 3286, 3504, 3729, 3961, 4200, 4446, 4699, 4959, 5226, 5500, 5781, 6069, 6364, 6666, 6975, 7291, 7614, 7944, 8281, 8625, 8976, 9334, 9699.

The parity of _____s follows the pattern odd-odd-even-even.

   a. Heptagonal pyramidal number
   b. Trillionth
   c. Ramanujan-Soldner constant
   d. Nonagonal number

28. George Pólya's 1945 book _____ is a small volume describing methods of problem solving.

This book was published at Princeton University. It suggests the following steps when solving a mathematical problem:

1. First, you have to understand the problem.
2. After understanding, then make a plan.
3. Carry out the plan.
4. Look back on your work. How could it be better?

If this technique fails, Pólya advises: 'If you can't solve a problem, then there is an easier problem you can solve: find it.' Or: 'If you cannot solve the proposed problem, try to solve first some related problem. Could you imagine a more accessible related problem?'

His book contains a dictionary-style set of heuristics, many of which have to do with generating a more accessible problem.

a. How to Solve It
b. Principia Mathematica
c. The Code Book
d. Categories for the Working Mathematician

29. A _____ or numeral palindrome is a 'symmetrical' number like 16461, that remains the same when its digits are reversed. The term palindromic is derived from palindrome, which refers to a word like rotor that remains unchanged under reversal of its letters. The first _____s are:

0, 1, 2, 3, 4, 5, 6, 7, 8, 9, 11, 22, 33, 44, 55, 66, 77, 88, 99, 101, 111, 121, 131, 141, 151, 161, 171, 181, 191, â€¦.

a. Harshad number
b. Permutable prime
c. Self number
d. Palindromic number

30. In World War II, _____ was the United States codename for intelligence derived from the cryptanalysis of PURPLE, a Japanese foreign office cipher.

The Japanese and the Germans both used the Enigma machine to encode their cable traffic. The Japanese Enigma-based system was called PURPLE by U.S. cryptographers.

a. Magic
b. Basis
c. Discontinuity
d. Bandwidth

31. In recreational mathematics, a _____ of order n is an arrangement of n^2 numbers, usually distinct integers, in a square, such that the n numbers in all rows, all columns, and both diagonals sum to the same constant. A normal _____ contains the integers from 1 to n^2. The term '_____' is also sometimes used to refer to any of various types of word square.
a. Prime reciprocal magic square
b. Magic square
c. 120-cell
d. 1-center problem

32. A _____ typically refers to a class of handheld calculators that are capable of plotting graphs, solving simultaneous equations, and performing numerous other tasks with variables. Most popular _____s are also programmable, allowing the user to create customized programs, typically for scientific/engineering and education applications. Due to their large displays intended for graphing, they can also accommodate several lines of text and calculations at a time.
a. Bump mapping
b. Genus
c. Support vector machines
d. Graphing calculator

33. A _____ is a deliberate process for transforming one or more inputs into one or more results, with variable change.

The term is used in a variety of senses, from the very definite arithmetical using an algorithm to the vague heuristics of calculating a strategy in a competition or calculating the chance of a successful relationship between two people.

Multiplying 7 by 8 is a simple algorithmic _____.

a. Mathematical maturity
b. Mathematics Subject Classification
c. Calculation
d. Mathematical object

34. A _____ is a device for performing mathematical calculations, distinguished from a computer by having a limited problem solving ability and an interface optimized for interactive calculation rather than programming. _____s can be hardware or software, and mechanical or electronic, and are often built into devices such as PDAs or mobile phones.

Modern electronic _____s are generally small, digital, and usually inexpensive.

a. 2-3 heap
b. Calculator
c. 1-center problem
d. 120-cell

35. The mathematical concept of a _____ expresses the intuitive idea of deterministic dependence between two quantities, one of which is viewed as primary and the other as secondary. A _____ then is a way to associate a unique output for each input of a specified type, for example, a real number or an element of a given set.

a. Coherent
b. Going up
c. Grill
d. Function

36. In mathematics, the _____ functions are functions of an angle; they are important when studying triangles and modeling periodic phenomena, among many other applications.

a. Coversine
b. Law of sines
c. Gudermannian function
d. Trigonometric

37. In mathematics, the _____ are functions of an angle. They are important in the study of triangles and modeling periodic phenomena, among many other applications. _____ are commonly defined as ratios of two sides of a right triangle containing the angle, and can equivalently be defined as the lengths of various line segments from a unit circle.

a. Trigonometric integrals
b. Sine
c. Law of sines
d. Trigonometric functions

38. A bar chart or _____ is a chart with rectangular bars with lengths proportional to the values that they represent. Bar charts are used for comparing two or more values. The bars can be horizontally or vertically oriented.

a. 2-3 heap
b. 120-cell
c. 1-center problem
d. Bar graph

39. _____ is the calculated approximation of a result which is usable even if input data may be incomplete or uncertain.

In statistics, see _____ theory, estimator.

In mathematics, approximation or _____ typically means finding upper or lower bounds of a quantity that cannot readily be computed precisely and is also an educated guess .

a. U-statistic
b. Estimator
c. Estimation
d. Estimation theory

40. In a graph theory, the _____ L

One of the earliest and most important theorems about _____s is due to Hassler Whitney, who proved that with one exceptional case the structure of G can be recovered completely from its _____.

- a. Bivariegated graph
- b. Vertex-transitive graph
- c. Sparse graph
- d. Line graph

41. A _____ is a circular chart divided into sectors, illustrating relative magnitudes or frequences or percents. In a _____, the arc length of each sector, is proportional to the quantity it represents. Together, the sectors create a full disk.
- a. 1-center problem
- b. 2-3 heap
- c. 120-cell
- d. Pie chart

42. In graph theory, a _____ in a graph is a sequence of vertices such that from each of its vertices there is an edge to the next vertex in the sequence. The first vertex is called the start vertex and the last vertex is called the end vertex. Both of them are called end or terminal vertices of the _____.
- a. Class
- b. Blinding
- c. Path
- d. Deltoid

43. _____ is the study of the principles of valid demonstration and inference. _____ is a branch of philosophy, a part of the classical trivium of grammar, _____, and rhetoric. of λογικÏŒς, 'possessed of reason, intellectual, dialectical, argumentative', from λÏŒγος logos, 'word, thought, idea, argument, account, reason, or principle'.
- a. Satisfiability
- b. Boolean function
- c. Counterpart theory
- d. Logic

44. A _____ is one of the basic shapes of geometry: a polygon with three corners or vertices and three sides or edges which are line segments. A _____ with vertices A, B, and C is denoted ABC.

In Euclidean geometry any three non-collinear points determine a unique _____ and a unique plane.

- a. Kepler triangle
- b. Fuhrmann circle
- c. 1-center problem
- d. Triangle

Chapter 2. The Basic Concepts of Set Theory

1. The term _____ in computer graphics and CAD systems is used in various senses, with common meaning of atomic geometric objects the system can handle. Sometimes the subroutines that draw the corresponding objects are called '_____s' as well. The most 'primitive' primitives are point and straight line segment, which were all that early vector graphics systems had.
   a. Geometric primitive
   b. Space partitioning
   c. High dynamic range rendering
   d. Solid modeling

2. _____ is a part of mathematics concerned with questions of size, shape, and relative position of figures and with properties of space. _____ is one of the oldest sciences. Initially a body of practical knowledge concerning lengths, areas, and volumes, in the third century BC _____ was put into an axiomatic form by Euclid, whose treatment--Euclidean _____--set a standard for many centuries to follow.
   a. 2-3 heap
   b. 120-cell
   c. 1-center problem
   d. Geometry

3. In geometry and trigonometry, an _____ is the figure formed by two rays sharing a common endpoint, called the vertex of the _____. The magnitude of the _____ is the 'amount of rotation' that separates the two rays, and can be measured by considering the length of circular arc swept out when one ray is rotated about the vertex to coincide with the other. Where there is no possibility of confusion, the term '_____' is used interchangeably for both the geometric configuration itself and for its angular magnitude.
   a. Angle
   b. A posteriori
   c. A chemical equation
   d. A Mathematical Theory of Communication

4. _____ is a technique used in solid modeling. CSG is often, but not always, a procedural modeling technique used in 3D computer graphics and CAD. _____ allows a modeler to create a complex surface or object by using Boolean operators to combine objects.
   a. Vertex shader
   b. Hidden surface determination
   c. Constructive solid Geometry
   d. Gouraud shading

5. In mathematics, _____ was the traditional name for the geometry of three-dimensional Euclidean space -- for practical purposes the kind of space we live in. It was developed following the development of plane geometry. Stereometry deals with the measurements of volumes of various solid figures: cylinder, circular cone, truncated cone, sphere, prisms, blades, wine casks.
   a. Three-dimensional space
   b. Solid Geometry
   c. Surface of constant width
   d. Steinmetz solid

6. In mathematics, _____ are generalized numbers used to measure the cardinality of sets. For finite sets, the cardinality is given by a natural number, which is simply the number of elements in the set. There are also transfinite _____ that describe the sizes of infinite sets.
   a. Strong partition cardinal
   b. Cardinality of the continuum
   c. Suslin cardinal
   d. Cardinal numbers

7. In mathematics, the _____ is a direct product of sets. The _____ is named after René Descartes, whose formulation of analytic geometry gave rise to this concept.

Specifically, the _____ of two sets X and Y, denoted X × Y, is the set of all possible ordered pairs whose first component is a member of X and whose second component is a member of Y:

$$X \times Y = \{(x,y) | x \in X \text{ and } y \in Y\}.$$

For example, the _____ of the 13-element set of standard playing card ranks {Ace, King, Queen, Jack, 10, 9, 8, 7, 6, 5, 4, 3, 2} and the four-element set of card suits {♠, ♥, ♦, ♣} is the 52-element set of all possible playing cards ,, ...,, ...,}.

  a. Choice function
  b. Set of all sets
  c. Disjoint sets
  d. Cartesian product

8. In mathematics, an _____ or member of a set is any one of the distinct objects that make up that set.

Writing A = {1,2,3,4}, means that the _____s of the set A are the numbers 1, 2, 3 and 4. Groups of _____s of A, for example {1,2}, are subsets of A.

  a. Universal code
  b. Element
  c. Order
  d. Ideal

9. In mathematics, the _____ of a set is a measure of the 'number of elements of the set'. For example, the set A = {1, 2, 3} contains 3 elements, and therefore A has a _____ of 3. There are two approaches to _____ - one which compares sets directly using bijections and injections, and another which uses cardinal numbers.
  a. Cardinality
  b. 1-center problem
  c. 2-3 heap
  d. 120-cell

10. In mathematics, a _____ can mean either an element of the set {1, 2, 3, ...} or an element of the set {0, 1, 2, 3, ...}. The latter is especially preferred in mathematical logic, set theory, and computer science.

_____s have two main purposes: they can be used for counting, and they can be used for ordering.

  a. Natural number
  b. Cardinal numbers
  c. Strong partition cardinal
  d. Suslin cardinal

11. In mathematics, and more specifically set theory, the _____ is the unique set having no members. Some axiomatic set theories assure that the _____ exists by including an axiom of _____; in other theories, its existence can be deduced. Many possible properties of sets are trivially true for the _____.
  a. Empty set
  b. Empty function
  c. A Mathematical Theory of Communication
  d. Inverse function

12. The _____ are the set of numbers consisting of the natural numbers including 0 and their negatives. They are numbers that can be written without a fractional or decimal component, and fall within the set {... −2, −1, 0, 1, 2, ...}.

Chapter 2. The Basic Concepts of Set Theory

    a. A chemical equation
    b. A posteriori
    c. A Mathematical Theory of Communication
    d. Integers

13. In mathematics, a _____ is a set that is negligible in some sense. For different applications, the meaning of 'negligible' varies. In measure theory, any set of measure 0 is called a _____.
    a. Radonifying function
    b. Borel-Cantelli lemma
    c. Prevalence and shyness
    d. Null set

14. In mathematics, a _____ is a number which can be expressed as a ratio of two integers. Non-integer _____s are usually written as the vulgar fraction $\frac{a}{b}$, where b is not zero. a is called the numerator, and b the denominator.
    a. Pre-algebra
    b. Rational number
    c. Minkowski distance
    d. Tally marks

15. In mathematics, the _____s may be described informally in several different ways. The _____s include both rational numbers, such as 42 and −23/129, and irrational numbers, such as pi and the square root of two; or, a _____ can be given by an infinite decimal representation, such as 2.4871773339...., where the digits continue in some way; or, the _____s may be thought of as points on an infinitely long number line.

These descriptions of the _____s, while intuitively accessible, are not sufficiently rigorous for the purposes of pure mathematics.

    a. Pre-algebra
    b. Minkowski distance
    c. Tally marks
    d. Real number

16. In mathematics, a _____ can mean either an element of the set {1, 2, 3, ...} (i.e the positive integers) or an element of the set {0, 1, 2, 3, ...} (i.e. the non-negative integers).
    a. Degrees of freedom
    b. Whole number
    c. Bounded
    d. FISH

17. In mathematics, the _____ of a real number is its numerical value without regard to its sign. So, for example, 3 is the _____ of both 3 and −3.

The _____ of a number a is denoted by $|a|$.

Generalizations of the _____ for real numbers occur in a wide variety of mathematical settings.

    a. Absolute value
    b. A Mathematical Theory of Communication
    c. A chemical equation
    d. Area hyperbolic functions

18. A _____ of a non-negative real number r is an expression of the form

$$r = \sum_{i=0}^{\infty} \frac{a_i}{10^i}$$

where a_0 is a nonnegative integer, and $a_1, a_2, \ldots$ are integers satisfying $0 \leq a_i \leq 9$; this is often written more briefly as

$$r = a_0.a_1 a_2 a_3 \ldots$$

That is to say, a_0 is the integer part of r, not necessarily between 0 and 9, and $a_1, a_2, a_3, \ldots$ are the digits forming the fractional part of r.

Any real number can be approximated to any desired degree of accuracy by rational numbers with finite _____s.

Assume $x \geq 0$. Then for every integer $n \geq 1$ there is a finite decimal $r_n = a_0.a_1 a_2 \cdots a_n$ such that

$$r_n \leq x < r_n + \frac{1}{10^n}.$$

Proof:

Let $r_n = \frac{p}{10^n}$, where $p = \lfloor 10^n x \rfloor$.

   a. Decimal representation   b. 1-center problem
   c. 2-3 heap   d. 120-cell

19. _____ is the state of being greater than any finite number, however large.
   a. A Mathematical Theory of Communication   b. Infinity
   c. Implicit differentiation   d. Interval notation

20. _____ (November 23, 1616 - October 28, 1703) was an English mathematician who is given partial credit for the development of modern calculus. Between 1643 and 1689 he served as chief cryptographer for Parliament and, later, the royal court. He is also credited with introducing the symbol ∞ for infinity.
   a. John Wallis   b. Matthew Foreman
   c. Carl R. de Boor   d. Maurice Kendall

21. _____ is the mathematical operation of scaling one number by another. It is one of the four basic operations in elementary arithmetic.

_____ is defined for whole numbers in terms of repeated addition; for example, 4 multiplied by 3 can be calculated by adding 3 copies of 4 together:

$$4 + 4 + 4 = 12.$$

Chapter 2. The Basic Concepts of Set Theory

_____ of rational numbers and real numbers is defined by systematic generalization of this basic idea.

a. Multiplication
b. Least common multiple
c. Highest common factor
d. The number 0 is even.

22. _____ is the likelihood or chance that something is the case or will happen. Theoretical _____ is used extensively in areas such as statistics, mathematics, science and philosophy to draw conclusions about the likelihood of potential events and the underlying mechanics of complex systems.

The word _____ does not have a consistent direct definition.

a. Standardized moment
b. Statistical significance
c. Probability
d. Discrete random variable

23. In mathematics, and particularly in applications to set theory and the foundations of mathematics, a _____ or universal class is a class that contains all of the elements and sets that one may wish to use in a given situation. There are several versions of this general idea, described in the following sections.

Perhaps the simplest version is that any set can be a _____, so long as the object of study is confined to that particular set.

a. Universe
b. A chemical equation
c. Operation
d. A Mathematical Theory of Communication

24. _____ or set diagrams are diagrams that show all hypothetically possible logical relations between a finite collection of sets. _____ were invented around 1880 by John Venn. They are used in many fields, including set theory, probability, logic, statistics, and computer science.

a. Venn diagrams
b. 1-center problem
c. 2-3 heap
d. 120-cell

25. A _____ is a 2D geometric symbolic representation of information according to some visualization technique. Sometimes, the technique uses a 3D visualization which is then projected onto the 2D surface. The word graph is sometimes used as a synonym for _____.

a. 2-3 heap
b. 120-cell
c. Diagram
d. 1-center problem

26. In mathematics, especially in set theory, a set A is a _____ of a set B if A is 'contained' inside B. Notice that A and B may coincide. The relationship of one set being a _____ of another is called inclusion.

a. Cartesian product
b. Subset
c. Horizontal line test
d. Set of all sets

Chapter 2. The Basic Concepts of Set Theory

27. In mathematics, an _____ is a statement about the relative size or order of two objects, or about whether they are the same or not

- The notation a < b means that a is less than b.
- The notation a > b means that a is greater than b.
- The notation a ≠ b means that a is not equal to b, but does not say that one is bigger than the other or even that they can be compared in size.

In all these cases, a is not equal to b, hence, '_____'.

These relations are known as strict _____

- The notation a ≤ b means that a is less than or equal to b;
- The notation a ≥ b means that a is greater than or equal to b;

An additional use of the notation is to show that one quantity is much greater than another, normally by several orders of magnitude.

- The notation a << b means that a is much less than b.
- The notation a >> b means that a is much greater than b.

If the sense of the _____ is the same for all values of the variables for which its members are defined, then the _____ is called an 'absolute' or 'unconditional' _____. If the sense of an _____ holds only for certain values of the variables involved, but is reversed or destroyed for other values of the variables, it is called a conditional _____.

An _____ may appear unsolvable because it only states whether a number is larger or smaller than another number; but it is possible to apply the same operations for equalities to inequalities. For example, to find x for the _____ 10x > 23 one would divide 23 by 10.

a. A chemical equation
b. A Mathematical Theory of Communication
c. A posteriori
d. Inequality

28. In set theory, a _____ is a partially ordered set such that for each t ∈ T, the set {s ∈ T : s < t} is well-ordered by the relation <. For each t ∈ T, the order type of {s ∈ T : s < t} is called the height of t. The height of T itself is the least ordinal greater than the height of each element of T.

a. Set-theoretic topology
b. Transitive reduction
c. Tree
d. Definable numbers

29. Induction or _____, sometimes called inductive logic, is the process of reasoning in which the premises of an argument are believed to support the conclusion but do not entail it;. Induction is a form of reasoning that makes generalizations based on individual instances. It is used to ascribe properties or relations to types based on an observation instance; or to formulate laws based on limited observations of recurring phenomenal patterns.

Chapter 2. The Basic Concepts of Set Theory

a. Intuitionistic logic
b. Idempotency of entailment
c. Affine logic
d. Inductive reasoning

30. In mathematics, hyperbolic n-space, denoted H^n, is the maximally symmetric, simply connected, n-dimensional Riemannian manifold with constant sectional curvature −1. _____ is the principal example of a space exhibiting hyperbolic geometry. It can be thought of as the negative-curvature analogue of the n-sphere.

a. Horocycle
b. Hyperbolic geometry
c. Margulis lemma
d. Hyperbolic space

31. In mathematics, the _____ of two sets A and B is the set that contains all elements of A that also belong to B, but no other elements.

For explanation of the symbols used in this article, refer to the table of mathematical symbols.

The _____ of A and B

The _____ of A and B is written 'A ∩ B'. Formally:

x is an element of A ∩ B if and only if
- x is an element of A and
- x is an element of B.

For example:
- The _____ of the sets {1, 2, 3} and {2, 3, 4} is {2, 3}.
- The number 9 is not in the _____ of the set of prime numbers {2, 3, 5, 7, 11, â€¦} and the set of odd numbers {1, 3, 5, 7, 9, 11, â€¦}.

If the _____ of two sets A and B is empty, that is they have no elements in common, then they are said to be disjoint, denoted: A ∩ B = ∅. For example the sets {1, 2} and {3, 4} are disjoint, written
{1, 2} ∩ {3, 4} = ∅.

a. Advice
b. Intersection
c. Order
d. Erlang

32. In mathematics, two sets are said to be disjoint if they have no element in common. For example, {1, 2, 3} and {4, 5, 6} are _____.

Formally, two sets A and B are disjoint if their intersection is the empty set.
wikimedia.org/math/b/3/5/b35d3befc06b831ff4d6cd63bf922efb.png">

This definition extends to any collection of sets.

a. Preimage
b. Subset
c. Horizontal line test
d. Disjoint sets

33. In set theory, the term _____ refers to a set operation used in the convergence of set elements to form a resultant set containing the elements of both sets. As a simple example, a _____ of two disjoint sets, which do not have elements in common results in a set containing all elements from both sets. A Venn diagram representing the _____ of sets A and B.
   a. Event
   b. Introduction
   c. Union
   d. UES

34. In mathematics and statistics, the _____ of a list of numbers is the sum of all of the list divided by the number of items in the list. If the list is a statistical population, then the mean of that population is called a population mean. If the list is a statistical sample, we call the resulting statistic a sample mean.
   a. Unsolved problems in statistics
   b. Analysis of variance
   c. Interval estimation
   d. Arithmetic mean

35. In mathematics, _____ is a property that a binary operation can have. It means that, within an expression containing two or more of the same associative operators in a row, the order that the operations are performed does not matter as long as the sequence of the operands is not changed. That is, rearranging the parentheses in such an expression will not change its value.
   a. Unital
   b. Associativity
   c. Algebraically closed
   d. Idempotence

36. In mathematics, and in particular in abstract algebra, distributivity is a property of binary operations that generalises the _____ law from elementary algebra.
   a. General linear group
   b. Closure with a twist
   c. Distributive
   d. Permutation

37. In mathematics, the term _____ has several different important meanings:

   - An _____ is an equality that remains true regardless of the values of any variables that appear within it, to distinguish it from an equality which is true under more particular conditions. For this, the 'triple bar' symbol ≡ is sometimes used.
   - In algebra, an _____ or _____ element of a set S with a binary operation Â· is an element e that, when combined with any element x of S, produces that same x. That is, eÂ·x = xÂ·e = x for all x in S.
      - The _____ function from a set S to itself, often denoted id or id_S, s the function such that i = x for all x in S. This function serves as the _____ element in the set of all functions from S to itself with respect to function composition.
      - In linear algebra, the _____ matrix of size n is the n-by-n square matrix with ones on the main diagonal and zeros elsewhere. This matrix serves as the _____ with respect to matrix multiplication.

A common example of the first meaning is the trigonometric _____

$$\sin^2 \theta + \cos^2 \theta = 1$$

which is true for all real values of θ, as opposed to

$$\cos\theta = 1,$$

which is true only for some values of θ, not all. For example, the latter equation is true when $\theta = 0$, false when $\theta = 2$

The concepts of 'additive _____' and 'multiplicative _____' are central to the Peano axioms. The number 0 is the 'additive _____' for integers, real numbers, and complex numbers. For the real numbers, for all $a \in \mathbb{R}$,

$$0 + a = a,$$

$$a + 0 = a,$$ and

$$0 + 0 = 0.$$

Similarly, The number 1 is the 'multiplicative _____' for integers, real numbers, and complex numbers.

- a. Action
- b. Identity
- c. ARIA
- d. Intersection

38. In mathematics, an _____ is a special type of element of a set with respect to a binary operation on that set. It leaves other elements unchanged when combined with them. This is used for groups and related concepts.
- a. Algebraically closed
- b. Universal algebra
- c. Arity
- d. Identity element

39. In statistics, _____ has two related meanings:

- the arithmetic _____.
- the expected value of a random variable, which is also called the population _____.

It is sometimes stated that the '_____' _____s average. This is incorrect if '_____' is taken in the specific sense of 'arithmetic _____' as there are different types of averages: the _____, median, and mode. For instance, average house prices almost always use the median value for the average.

For a real-valued random variable X, the _____ is the expectation of X.

- a. Probability
- b. Mean
- c. Statistical population
- d. Proportional hazards model

Chapter 2. The Basic Concepts of Set Theory

40. In quantum field theory and statistical mechanics in the thermodynamic limit, a system with a global symmetry can have more than one phase. For parameters where the symmetry is spontaneously broken, the system is said to be _____. When the global symmetry is unbroken the system is disordered.
   a. Isoenthalpic-isobaric ensemble
   b. Ursell function
   c. Ordered
   d. Einstein relation

41. In mathematics, an _____ is a collection of objects having two coordinates (or entries or projections), such that one can always uniquely determine the object, which is the first coordinate (or first entry or left projection) of the pair as well as the second coordinate (or second entry or right projection.) If the first coordinate is a and the second is b, the usual notation for an _____ is (a, b.) The pair is 'ordered' in that (a, b) differs from (b, a) unless a = b.
   a. Ordered pair
   b. A chemical equation
   c. A Mathematical Theory of Communication
   d. A posteriori

42. The x-axis is the horizontal axis of a two-dimensional plot in the _____, that is typically pointed to the right. Also known as a right-handed coordinate system.
   a. 120-cell
   b. Cartesian coordinate system
   c. 1-center problem
   d. 2-3 heap

43. In mathematics and in the sciences, a _____ (plural: _____e, formulæ or _____s) is a concise way of expressing information symbolically (as in a mathematical or chemical _____), or a general relationship between quantities. One of many famous _____e is Albert Einstein's E = mc² (see special relativity

In mathematics, a _____ is a key to solve an equation with variables. For example, the problem of determining the volume of a sphere is one that requires a significant amount of integral calculus to solve.

   a. 120-cell
   b. 1-center problem
   c. 2-3 heap
   d. Formula

44. In the study of metric spaces in mathematics, there are various notions of two metrics on the same underlying space being 'the same', or _____.

In the following, M will denote a non-empty set and d_1 and d_2 will denote two metrics on M.

The two metrics d_1 and d_2 are said to be topologically _____ if they generate the same topology on M.

   a. A posteriori
   b. A chemical equation
   c. Equivalent
   d. A Mathematical Theory of Communication

Chapter 3. Introduction to Logic

1. A _____ is a 2D geometric symbolic representation of information according to some visualization technique. Sometimes, the technique uses a 3D visualization which is then projected onto the 2D surface. The word graph is sometimes used as a synonym for _____.
    a. 2-3 heap
    b. 120-cell
    c. 1-center problem
    d. Diagram

2. _____ is the study of the principles of valid demonstration and inference. _____ is a branch of philosophy, a part of the classical trivium of grammar, _____, and rhetoric. of λογικῆς, 'possessed of reason, intellectual, dialectical, argumentative', from λΐŒγος logos, 'word, thought, idea, argument, account, reason, or principle'.
    a. Boolean function
    b. Counterpart theory
    c. Satisfiability
    d. Logic

3. In logic and mathematics, _____ or not is an operation on logical values, for example, the logical value of a proposition, that sends true to false and false to true. Intuitively, the _____ of a proposition holds exactly when that proposition does not hold. In grammar, nor is an adverb which acts as a coordinating conjunction.
    a. Negation
    b. Syntax
    c. Sentence diagram
    d. 1-center problem

4. In mathematics, a _____ can mean either an element of the set {1, 2, 3, ...} or an element of the set {0, 1, 2, 3, ...}. The latter is especially preferred in mathematical logic, set theory, and computer science.

    _____s have two main purposes: they can be used for counting, and they can be used for ordering.

    a. Natural number
    b. Strong partition cardinal
    c. Cardinal numbers
    d. Suslin cardinal

5. In mathematics, a _____ is a number which can be expressed as a ratio of two integers. Non-integer _____s are usually written as the vulgar fraction $\frac{a}{b}$, where b is not zero. a is called the numerator, and b the denominator.
    a. Pre-algebra
    b. Tally marks
    c. Minkowski distance
    d. Rational number

6. In mathematics, the _____s may be described informally in several different ways. The _____s include both rational numbers, such as 42 and −23/129, and irrational numbers, such as pi and the square root of two; or, a _____ can be given by an infinite decimal representation, such as 2.4871773339...., where the digits continue in some way; or, the _____s may be thought of as points on an infinitely long number line.

    These descriptions of the _____s, while intuitively accessible, are not sufficiently rigorous for the purposes of pure mathematics.

    a. Tally marks
    b. Minkowski distance
    c. Real number
    d. Pre-algebra

7. In mathematics, a _____ can mean either an element of the set {1, 2, 3, ...} (i.e the positive integers) or an element of the set {0, 1, 2, 3, ...} (i.e. the non-negative integers).

a. Whole number
c. FISH
b. Bounded
d. Degrees of freedom

8. In mathematics, the _____ of a real number is its numerical value without regard to its sign. So, for example, 3 is the _____ of both 3 and −3.

The _____ of a number a is denoted by $|a|$.

Generalizations of the _____ for real numbers occur in a wide variety of mathematical settings.

a. A Mathematical Theory of Communication
c. A chemical equation
b. Area hyperbolic functions
d. Absolute value

9. A _____ of a non-negative real number r is an expression of the form

$$r = \sum_{i=0}^{\infty} \frac{a_i}{10^i}$$

where a_0 is a nonnegative integer, and $a_1, a_2, \ldots$ are integers satisfying $0 \leq a_i \leq 9$; this is often written more briefly as

$$r = a_0.a_1 a_2 a_3 \ldots$$

That is to say, a_0 is the integer part of r, not necessarily between 0 and 9, and $a_1, a_2, a_3, \ldots$ are the digits forming the fractional part of r.

Any real number can be approximated to any desired degree of accuracy by rational numbers with finite _____ s.

Assume $x \geq 0$. Then for every integer $n \geq 1$ there is a finite decimal $r_n = a_0.a_1 a_2 \cdots a_n$ such that

$$r_n \leq x < r_n + \frac{1}{10^n}.$$

Proof:

Let $r_n = \frac{p}{10^n}$, where $p = \lfloor 10^n x \rfloor$.

a. 1-center problem
c. Decimal representation
b. 120-cell
d. 2-3 heap

Chapter 3. Introduction to Logic

10. In logic and mathematics, or, also known as logical _____ or inclusive _____ is a logical operator that results in true whenever one or more of its operands are true. In grammar, or is a coordinating conjunction. In ordinary language 'or' rather has the meaning of exclusive _____.

   a. Cube
   b. Zero-point energy
   c. Triquetra
   d. Disjunction

11. A _____ is a mathematical table used in logic -- specifically in connection with Boolean algebra, boolean functions, and propositional calculus -- to compute the functional values of logical expressions on each of their functional arguments, that is, on each combination of values taken by their logical variables. In particular, _____s can be used to tell whether a propositional expression is true for all legitimate input values, that is, logically valid.

The pattern of reasoning that the _____ tabulates was Frege's, Peirce's, and Schröder's by 1880.

   a. 120-cell
   b. 1-center problem
   c. 2-3 heap
   d. Truth table

12. In logic, two sentences (either in a formal language or a natural language) may be joined by means of a _____ to form a compound sentence. The truth-value of the compound is uniquely determined by the truth-values of the simpler sentences. The _____ therefore represents a function, and since the value of the compound sentence is a truth-value, it is called a truth-function and the _____ is called a 'truth-functional connective'.

   a. Satisfiability
   b. Set theory
   c. Fallacies of definition
   d. Logical connective

13. Induction or _____, sometimes called inductive logic, is the process of reasoning in which the premises of an argument are believed to support the conclusion but do not entail it;. Induction is a form of reasoning that makes generalizations based on individual instances. It is used to ascribe properties or relations to types based on an observation instance; or to formulate laws based on limited observations of recurring phenomenal patterns.

   a. Affine logic
   b. Intuitionistic logic
   c. Idempotency of entailment
   d. Inductive reasoning

14. In mathematics, hyperbolic n-space, denoted H^n, is the maximally symmetric, simply connected, n-dimensional Riemannian manifold with constant sectional curvature −1. _____ is the principal example of a space exhibiting hyperbolic geometry. It can be thought of as the negative-curvature analogue of the n-sphere.

   a. Horocycle
   b. Margulis lemma
   c. Hyperbolic geometry
   d. Hyperbolic space

15. In the study of metric spaces in mathematics, there are various notions of two metrics on the same underlying space being 'the same', or _____.

In the following, M will denote a non-empty set and d_1 and d_2 will denote two metrics on M.

The two metrics d_1 and d_2 are said to be topologically _____ if they generate the same topology on M.

a. Equivalent
b. A posteriori
c. A Mathematical Theory of Communication
d. A chemical equation

16. In mathematics, the _____ of a number n is the number that, when added to n, yields zero. The _____ of n is denoted −n. For example, 7 is −7, because 7 + (−7) = 0, and the _____ of −0.3 is 0.3, because −0.3 + 0.3 = 0.

a. Associativity
b. Algebraic structure
c. Arity
d. Additive inverse

17. The _____ is a 3-volume work on the foundations of mathematics, written by Alfred North Whitehead and Bertrand Russell and published in 1910-1913. It is an attempt to derive all mathematical truths from a well-defined set of axioms and inference rules in symbolic logic. One of the main inspirations and motivations for the Principia was Frege's earlier work on logic, which had led to paradoxes discovered by Russell.

a. Visible
b. Social Choice and Individual Values
c. To Mock a Mockingbird
d. Principia Mathematica

18. _____ is the field of mathematics that studies algebraic structures themselves, not examples of algebraic structures. For instance, rather than take particular groups as the object of study, in _____ one takes 'the theory of groups' as an object of study.

From the point of view of _____, an algebra is a set A together with a collection of operations on A.

a. Ordered exponential
b. Anticommutativity
c. Arity
d. Universal Algebra

19. In cryptography, _____ is a pseudorandom number generator and a stream cipher designed by Robert Jenkins to be cryptographically secure. The name is an acronym for Indirection, Shift, Accumulate, Add, and Count.

The _____ algorithm has similarities with RC4.

a. Introduction
b. Order
c. Isaac
d. Imputation

20. The _____ (symbol: N) is the SI derived unit of force, named after Isaac _____ in recognition of his work on classical mechanics.

The _____ is the unit of force derived in the SI system; it is equal to the amount of force required to accelerate a mass of one kilogram at a rate of one meter per second per second. Algebraically:

$$1\text{ N} = 1\ \frac{\text{kg}\cdot\text{m}}{\text{s}^2}.$$

- 1 N is the force of Earth's gravity on an object with a mass of about 102 g ($\frac{1}{9.8}$ kg) (such as a small apple.)
- On Earth's surface, a mass of 1 kg exerts a force of approximately 9.80665 N [down] (or 1 kgf.) The approximation of 1 kg corresponding to 10 N is sometimes used as a rule of thumb in everyday life and in engineering.
- The force of Earth's gravity on a human being with a mass of 70 kg is approximately 687 N.
- The dot product of force and distance is mechanical work. Thus, in SI units, a force of 1 N exerted over a distance of 1 m is 1 NÂ·m of work. The Work-Energy Theorem states that the work done on a body is equal to the change in energy of the body. 1 NÂ·m = 1 J (joule), the SI unit of energy.
- It is common to see forces expressed in kilonewtons or kN, where 1 kN = 1 000 N.

a. 120-cell
b. 1-center problem
c. 2-3 heap
d. Newton

21. In mathematics, an _____ or member of a set is any one of the distinct objects that make up that set.

Writing A = {1,2,3,4}, means that the _____s of the set A are the numbers 1, 2, 3 and 4. Groups of _____s of A, for example {1,2}, are subsets of A.

a. Element
b. Order
c. Ideal
d. Universal code

Chapter 4. Numeration and Mathematical Systems

1. In mathematics, computing, linguistics and related subjects, an _____ is a sequence of finite instructions, often used for calculation and data processing. It is formally a type of effective method in which a list of well-defined instructions for completing a task will, when given an initial state, proceed through a well-defined series of successive states, eventually terminating in an end-state. The transition from one state to the next is not necessarily deterministic; some _____s, known as probabilistic _____s, incorporate randomness.

   a. Approximate counting algorithm
   b. Out-of-core
   c. In-place algorithm
   d. Algorithm

2. In discrete mathematics and predominantly in set theory, a _____ is a concept used in comparisons of sets to refer to the unique values of one set in relation to another. The terms 'absolute' and 'relative' _____ refer to more specific applications of the concept, with universal _____s referring to elements unique to the universal set and the latter referring to the unique elements of one set in relation to another. In this image, the universal set is represented by the border of the image, and the set A as a disc.

   a. Derivative algebra
   b. Huge
   c. Kernel
   d. Complement

3. A _____ is a form of rhombus. The definition of _____ is not strictly fixed, and it is sometimes used simply as a synonym for rhombus. Most often, though, _____ refers to a thin rhombus -- a rhombus with acute angles of 45°.

   a. Trapezium
   b. Trapezoid
   c. Rhomboid
   d. Lozenge

4. _____ is the title of a short book on logic by Gottlob Frege, published in 1879, and is also the name of the formal system set out in that book.

   _____ is usually translated as concept writing or concept notation; the full title of the book identifies it as 'a formula language, modelled on that of arithmetic, of pure thought.' The _____ was arguably the most important publication in logic since Aristotle founded the subject. Frege's motivation for developing his formal approach to logic resembled Leibniz's motivation for his calculus ratiocinator.

   a. 2-3 heap
   b. 1-center problem
   c. 120-cell
   d. Begriffsschrift

5. In mathematics and computer science, _____ (also base-16, hexa or base, of 16. It uses sixteen distinct symbols, most often the symbols 0-9 to represent values zero to nine, and A, B, C, D, E, F (or a through f) to represent values ten to fifteen.

   Its primary use is as a human friendly representation of binary coded values, so it is often used in digital electronics and computer engineering.

   a. Radix
   b. Tetradecimal
   c. Factoradic
   d. Hexadecimal

6. Exponentiation is a mathematical operation, written a^n, involving two numbers, the base a and the _____ n. When n is a positive integer, exponentiation corresponds to repeated multiplication:

$$a^n = \underbrace{a \times \cdots \times a}_{n},$$

just as multiplication by a positive integer corresponds to repeated addition:

$$a \times n = \underbrace{a + \cdots + a}_{n}.$$

The _____ is usually shown as a superscript to the right of the base. The exponentiation a^n can be read as: a raised to the n-th power, a raised to the power [of] n or possibly a raised to the _____ [of] n, or more briefly: a to the n-th power or a to the power [of] n, or even more briefly: a to the n.

a. Exponential sum
b. Exponential tree
c. Exponentiating by squaring
d. Exponent

7. A _____ is a software program that facilitates symbolic mathematics. The core functionality of a CAS is manipulation of mathematical expressions in symbolic form.

The symbolic manipulations supported typically include

- simplification to the smallest possible expression or some standard form, including automatic simplification with assumptions and simplification with constraints
- substitution of symbolic, functors or numeric values for expressions
- change of form of expressions: expanding products and powers, partial and full factorization, rewriting as partial fractions, constraint satisfaction, rewriting trigonometric functions as exponentials, etc.
- partial and total differentiation
- symbolic constrained and unconstrained global optimization
- solution of linear and some non-linear equations over various domains
- solution of some differential and difference equations
- taking some limits
- some indefinite and definite integration, including multidimensional integrals
- integral transforms
- arbitrary-precision numeric operations
- Series operations such as expansion, summation and products
- matrix operations including products, inverses, etc.
- display of mathematical expressions in two-dimensional mathematical form, often using typesetting systems similar to TeX
- add-ons for use in applied mathematics such as physics packages for physical computation
- plotting graphs and parametric plots of functions in two and three dimensions, and animating them
- APIs for linking it on an external program such as a database, or using in a programming language to use the _____
- drawing charts and diagrams
- string manipulation such as matching and searching
- statistical computation
- Theorem proving and verification
- graphic production and editing such as CGI and signal processing as image processing
- sound synthesis

Many also include a programming language, allowing users to implement their own algorithms.

Some _____s focus on a specific area of application; these are typically developed in academia and are free.

a. 2-3 heap
c. 120-cell
b. 1-center problem
d. Computer algebra system

8. _____, as that term is used in this article, is the mathematics written in Greek, developed from the 6th century BC to the 5th century AD around the Eastern shores of the Mediterranean. The word 'mathematics' itself derives from the ancient Greek μαθημα, meaning 'subject of instruction'.. The study of mathematics for its own sake and the use of generalized mathematical theories and proofs is the key difference between _____ and those of preceding civilizations.

Chapter 4. Numeration and Mathematical Systems

a. 2-3 heap
b. 120-cell
c. 1-center problem
d. Greek mathematics

9. _____ refers to any mathematics of the peoples of Mesopotamia, from the days of the early Sumerians to the fall of Babylon in 539 BC. In contrast to the scarcity of sources in Egyptian mathematics, our knowledge of _____ is derived from some 400 clay tablets unearthed since the 1850s. Written in Cuneiform script, tablets were inscribed while the clay was moist, and baked hard in an oven or by the heat of the sun.

a. 120-cell
b. 1-center problem
c. Babylonian mathematics
d. 2-3 heap

10. The term _____ refers to the central sense organ complex, for those animals that have one, normally on the ventral surface of the head and can depending on the definition in the human case, include the hair, forehead, eyebrow, eyes, nose, ears, cheeks, mouth, lips, philtrum, teeth, skin, and chin. The _____ has uses of expression, appearance, and identity amongst others.It also has different senses like smelling, tasting, hearing, and seeing.

Caricatures often exaggerate facial features to make a _____ more easily recognized in association with a pronounced portion of the _____ of the individual in question--for example, a caricature of Osama bin Laden might focus on his facial hair and nose; a caricature of George W. Bush might enlarge his ears to the size of an elephant¢s; a caricature of Jay Leno may pronounce his head and chin; and a caricature of Mick Jagger might enlarge his lips.

a. 1-center problem
b. 120-cell
c. Face
d. 2-3 heap

11. _____ is a numeral system in which each position is related to the next by a constant multiplier, a common ratio, called the base or radix of that numeral system.

a. Cyrillic numerals
b. NegaFibonacci coding
c. Negative base
d. Place value

12. Leonardo of Pisa (c. 1170 - c. 1250), also known as Leonardo Pisano, Leonardo Bonacci, Leonardo _____, or, most commonly, simply _____, was an Italian mathematician, considered by some 'the most talented mathematician of the Middle Ages'.

a. Guido Castelnuovo
b. Harry Hinsley
c. Ralph C. Merkle
d. Fibonacci

13. In cryptography, the _____ was a method devised by Polish mathematician-cryptologist Jerzy Różycki, at the Polish General Staff's Cipher Bureau, to facilitate decrypting German Enigma messages. This method sometimes made it possible to determine which of the Enigma machine's rotors was at the far right, that is, in the position where the rotor always revolved at every depression of a key.

- Biuro Szyfrów

a. FROSTBURG
b. TWIRL
c. Bombe
d. Clock

14. In mathematics, the _____ is a term used to describe the number of times one must apply a given operation to an integer before reaching a fixed point.

Usually, this refers to the additive or multiplicative persistence of an integer, which is how often one has to replace the number by the sum or product of its digits until one reaches a single digit. Because the numbers are broken down into their digits, the additive or multiplicative persistence depends on the radix.

   a. Persistence of a number
   b. Linear congruence theorem
   c. Lychrel number
   d. Coprime

15. In mathematics, and in particular in abstract algebra, distributivity is a property of binary operations that generalises the _____ law from elementary algebra.
   a. Closure with a twist
   b. General linear group
   c. Permutation
   d. Distributive

16. An _____ is a calculating tool used primarily in parts of Asia for performing arithmetic processes. Today, abaci are often constructed as a bamboo frame with beads sliding on wires, but originally they were beans or stones moved in grooves in sand or on tablets of wood, stone, or metal. The _____ was in use centuries before the adoption of the written modern numeral system and is still widely used by merchants, traders and clerks in Asia, Japan, Africa, India and elsewhere.
   a. A posteriori
   b. A chemical equation
   c. A Mathematical Theory of Communication
   d. Abacus

17. The _____ is a positional numeral system; it has positions for units, tens, hundreds, etc. The position of each digit conveys the multiplier (a power of ten) to be used with that digit—each position has a value ten times that of the position to its right.
   a. Composite
   b. Decimal system
   c. Free
   d. Cleaver

18. _____ is the mathematical operation of scaling one number by another. It is one of the four basic operations in elementary arithmetic.

_____ is defined for whole numbers in terms of repeated addition; for example, 4 multiplied by 3 can be calculated by adding 3 copies of 4 together:

$$4 + 4 + 4 = 12.$$

_____ of rational numbers and real numbers is defined by systematic generalization of this basic idea.

   a. The number 0 is even.
   b. Least common multiple
   c. Highest common factor
   d. Multiplication

19. In mathematics, especially in geometry and group theory, a _____ in R^n is a discrete subgroup of R^n which spans the real vector space R^n. Every _____ in R^n can be generated from a basis for the vector space by forming all linear combinations with integral coefficients. A _____ may be viewed as a regular tiling of a space by a primitive cell.

a. Homogeneity
b. Group
c. Boundary
d. Lattice

20. In mathematics, the _____ of a number to a given base is the power or exponent to which the base must be raised in order to produce the number.

For example, the _____ of 1000 to the base 10 is 3, because 3 is how many 10s one must multiply to get 1000: thus 10 × 10 × 10 = 1000; the base-2 _____ of 32 is 5 because 5 is how many 2s one must multiply to get 32: thus 2 × 2 × 2 × 2 × 2 = 32. In the language of exponents: $10^3 = 1000$, so $\log_{10} 1000 = 3$, and $2^5 = 32$, so $\log_2 32 = 5$.

   a. 120-cell
   b. Logarithm
   c. 1-center problem
   d. 2-3 heap

21. A _____ typically refers to a class of handheld calculators that are capable of plotting graphs, solving simultaneous equations, and performing numerous other tasks with variables. Most popular _____s are also programmable, allowing the user to create customized programs, typically for scientific/engineering and education applications. Due to their large displays intended for graphing, they can also accommodate several lines of text and calculations at a time.
   a. Support vector machines
   b. Graphing calculator
   c. Bump mapping
   d. Genus

22. A _____ is a device for performing mathematical calculations, distinguished from a computer by having a limited problem solving ability and an interface optimized for interactive calculation rather than programming. _____s can be hardware or software, and mechanical or electronic, and are often built into devices such as PDAs or mobile phones.

Modern electronic _____s are generally small, digital, and usually inexpensive.

   a. Calculator
   b. 1-center problem
   c. 2-3 heap
   d. 120-cell

23. The mathematical concept of a _____ expresses the intuitive idea of deterministic dependence between two quantities, one of which is viewed as primary and the other as secondary. A _____ then is a way to associate a unique output for each input of a specified type, for example, a real number or an element of a given set.
   a. Coherent
   b. Going up
   c. Function
   d. Grill

24. In mathematics, the _____ functions are functions of an angle; they are important when studying triangles and modeling periodic phenomena, among many other applications.
   a. Coversine
   b. Trigonometric
   c. Gudermannian function
   d. Law of sines

25. In mathematics, the _____ are functions of an angle. They are important in the study of triangles and modeling periodic phenomena, among many other applications. _____ are commonly defined as ratios of two sides of a right triangle containing the angle, and can equivalently be defined as the lengths of various line segments from a unit circle.

a. Sine
b. Trigonometric functions
c. Law of sines
d. Trigonometric integrals

26. The _____ numeral system is the base-8 number system, and uses the digits 0 to 7. Numerals can be made from binary numerals by grouping consecutive digits into groups of three (starting from the right.) For example, the binary representation for decimal 74 is 1001010, which groups into 001 001 010 -- so the _____ representation is 112.
   a. A posteriori
   b. Octal
   c. A Mathematical Theory of Communication
   d. A chemical equation

27. In mathematics, _____ is a property that a binary operation can have. It means that, within an expression containing two or more of the same associative operators in a row, the order that the operations are performed does not matter as long as the sequence of the operands is not changed. That is, rearranging the parentheses in such an expression will not change its value.
   a. Idempotence
   b. Algebraically closed
   c. Unital
   d. Associativity

28. In mathematics, a set is said to be _____ if the operation on members of the set produces a member of the set. For example, the real numbers are closed under subtraction, but the natural numbers are not: 3 and 7 are both natural numbers, but the result of 3 − 7 is not.

Similarly, a set is said to be closed under a collection of operations if it is closed under each of the operations individually.

   a. Contingency table
   b. Continuous linear extension
   c. Closed under some operation
   d. Control chart

29. The _____ is a rule which states that when you add or multiply numbers, changing the order doesn't change the result.
   a. Coimage
   b. Conditional event algebra
   c. Semigroupoid
   d. Commutative law

30. In mathematics, the term _____ has several different important meanings:

   - An _____ is an equality that remains true regardless of the values of any variables that appear within it, to distinguish it from an equality which is true under more particular conditions. For this, the 'triple bar' symbol ≡ is sometimes used.
   - In algebra, an _____ or _____ element of a set S with a binary operation Â· is an element e that, when combined with any element x of S, produces that same x. That is, eÂ·x = xÂ·e = x for all x in S.
     - The _____ function from a set S to itself, often denoted id or id_S, s the function such that i = x for all x in S. This function serves as the _____ element in the set of all functions from S to itself with respect to function composition.
     - In linear algebra, the _____ matrix of size n is the n-by-n square matrix with ones on the main diagonal and zeros elsewhere. This matrix serves as the _____ with respect to matrix multiplication.

Chapter 4. Numeration and Mathematical Systems

A common example of the first meaning is the trigonometric _____

$$\sin^2 \theta + \cos^2 \theta = 1$$

which is true for all real values of θ, as opposed to

$$\cos \theta = 1,$$

which is true only for some values of θ, not all. For example, the latter equation is true when $\theta = 0$, false when $\theta = 2$

The concepts of 'additive _____' and 'multiplicative _____' are central to the Peano axioms. The number 0 is the 'additive _____' for integers, real numbers, and complex numbers. For the real numbers, for all $a \in \mathbb{R}$,

$$0 + a = a,$$

$$a + 0 = a, \text{ and}$$

$$0 + 0 = 0.$$

Similarly, The number 1 is the 'multiplicative _____' for integers, real numbers, and complex numbers.

- a. Intersection
- b. Action
- c. Identity
- d. ARIA

31. In mathematics, the _____ of a number n is the number that, when added to n, yields zero. The _____ of n is denoted −n. For example, 7 is −7, because 7 + (−7) = 0, and the _____ of −0.3 is 0.3, because −0.3 + 0.3 = 0.
    - a. Additive inverse
    - b. Arity
    - c. Algebraic structure
    - d. Associativity

32. An _____ is a group satisfying the requirement that the product of elements does not depend on their order. _____s generalize the arithmetic of addition of integers; they are named after Niels Henrik Abel.

The concept of an _____ is one of the first concepts encountered in undergraduate abstract algebra, with many other basic objects, such as a module and a vector space, being its refinements.

- a. Algebraically compact
- b. Abelian group
- c. A Mathematical Theory of Communication
- d. Elementary abelian group

34 *Chapter 4. Numeration and Mathematical Systems*

33. In mathematics, a _____ is an algebraic structure consisting of a set together with an operation that combines any two of its elements to form a third element. To qualify as a _____, the set and operation must satisfy a few conditions called _____ axioms, namely associativity, identity and invertibility. While these are familiar from many mathematical structures, such as number systems--for example, the integers endowed with the addition operation form a _____--the formulation of the axioms is detached from the concrete nature of the _____ and its operation.
   a. Coherence
   b. Derivative algebra
   c. Characteristic function
   d. Group

34. _____ generally conveys two primary meanings. The first is an imprecise sense of harmonious or aesthetically-pleasing proportionality and balance; such that it reflects beauty or perfection. The second meaning is a precise and well-defined concept of balance or 'patterned self-similarity' that can be demonstrated or proved according to the rules of a formal system: by geometry, through physics or otherwise.
   a. Symmetry breaking
   b. Molecular symmetry
   c. Symmetry
   d. Tessellation

35. A _____ is a collection of data, usually presented in tabular form. Each column represents a particular variable. Each row corresponds to a given member of the _____ in question.
   a. 2-3 heap
   b. 120-cell
   c. 1-center problem
   d. Data set

36. In the mathematical field of group theory, the _____ M or F_1 is a group of finite order

   $2^{46} \cdot 3^{20} \cdot 5^9 \cdot 7^6 \cdot 11^2 \cdot 13^3 \cdot 17 \cdot 19 \cdot 23 \cdot 29 \cdot 31 \cdot 41 \cdot 47 \cdot 59 \cdot 71$
   = 808017424794512875886459904961710757005754368000000000
   $\approx 8 \cdot 10^{53}$.

It is a simple group, meaning it does not have any normal subgroups except for the subgroup consisting only of the identity element, and M itself.

The finite simple groups have been completely classified.

   a. Held group
   b. Monster group
   c. Rudvalis group
   d. Mathieu groups

37. In several fields of mathematics the term _____ is used with different but closely related meanings. They all relate to the notion of mapping the elements of a set to other elements of the same set, i.e., exchanging elements of a set.

The general concept of _____ can be defined more formally in different contexts:

In combinatorics, a _____ is usually understood to be a sequence containing each element from a finite set once, and only once.

   a. Linearly independent
   b. Cyclic permutation
   c. Tensor product
   d. Permutation

38. In mathematics, a _____ is a group G whose elements are permutations of a given set M, and whose group operation is the composition of permutations in G; the relationship is often written as. Note that the group of all permutations of a set is the symmetric group; the term _____ is usually restricted to mean a subgroup of the symmetric group. The symmetric group of n elements is denoted by S_n; if M is any finite or infinite set, then the group of all permutations of M is often written as Sy.

   a. Primitive permutation group   b. 1-center problem
   c. Parker vector   d. Permutation group

Chapter 5. Number Theory

1. _____ is a theoretical computer scientist and professor of computer science and molecular biology at the University of Southern California. He is known for being a co-inventor of the RSA cryptosystem in 1977, and of DNA computing. RSA is in widespread use in security applications, including https.

   a. Harold Hall 'Doc' Keen
   b. William Kingdon Clifford
   c. Johann Karl August Radon
   d. Leonard Max Adleman

2. In information theory, a _____ is a function mapping an alphabet to non-negative real numbers, satisfying a generalization of Kraft's inequality. A _____ page, a type of character encoding table, is one such _____.

   a. File Camouflage
   b. Deterministic encryption
   c. Link encryption
   d. Code

3. In mathematics, a _____ can mean either an element of the set {1, 2, 3, ...} or an element of the set {0, 1, 2, 3, ...}. The latter is especially preferred in mathematical logic, set theory, and computer science.

   _____s have two main purposes: they can be used for counting, and they can be used for ordering.

   a. Natural number
   b. Strong partition cardinal
   c. Cardinal numbers
   d. Suslin cardinal

4. In mathematics, a _____ of an integer n is an integer which evenly divides n without leaving a remainder.

   For example, 7 is a _____ of 42 because 42/7 = 6. We also say 42 is divisible by 7 or 42 is a multiple of 7 or 7 divides 42 or 7 is a factor of 42 and we usually write 7 | 42.

   a. 120-cell
   b. 2-3 heap
   c. 1-center problem
   d. Divisor

5. _____ is the branch of pure mathematics concerned with the properties of numbers in general, and integers in particular, as well as the wider classes of problems that arise from their study.

   _____ may be subdivided into several fields, according to the methods used and the type of questions investigated.

   The term 'arithmetic' is also used to refer to _____.

   a. Goormaghtigh conjecture
   b. Sociable number
   c. Coin problem
   d. Number theory

6. In cryptography, the _____ was a method devised by Polish mathematician-cryptologist Jerzy Różycki, at the Polish General Staff's Cipher Bureau, to facilitate decrypting German Enigma messages. This method sometimes made it possible to determine which of the Enigma machine's rotors was at the far right, that is, in the position where the rotor always revolved at every depression of a key.

   - Biuro Szyfrów

Chapter 5. Number Theory

a. TWIRL
c. FROSTBURG
b. Bombe
d. Clock

7. In mathematics, _____ is a system of arithmetic for integers, where numbers 'wrap around' after they reach a certain value -- the modulus. _____ was introduced by Carl Friedrich Gauss in his book Disquisitiones Arithmeticae, published in 1801.

A familiar use of _____ is its use in the 24-hour clock: the arithmetic of time-keeping in which the day runs from midnight to midnight and is divided into 24 hours, numbered from 0 to 23.

a. Discrete logarithm
c. Multiplicative group of integers modulo n
b. Residue number system
d. Modular arithmetic

8. A _____ number is a positive integer which has a positive divisor other than one or itself. By definition, every integer greater than one is either a prime number or a _____ number. zero and one are considered to be neither prime nor _____. For example, the integer 14 is a _____ number because it can be factored as 2 × 7.

a. Key server
c. Discontinuity
b. Basis
d. Composite

9. A _____ is a positive integer which has a positive divisor other than one or itself. In other words, if 0 < n is an integer and there are integers 1 < a, b < n such that n = a × b then n is composite. By definition, every integer greater than one is either a prime number or a _____.

a. Composite number
c. Ruth-Aaron pair
b. Prime Pages
d. Megaprime

10. In mathematics, a _____ is a mathematical statement which appears resourceful, but has not been formally proven to be true under the rules of mathematical logic. Once a _____ is formally proven true it is elevated to the status of theorem and may be used afterwards without risk in the construction of other formal mathematical proofs. Until that time, mathematicians may use the _____ on a provisional basis, but any resulting work is itself provisional until the underlying _____ is cleared up.

a. Moral certainty
c. Heawood conjecture
b. Conjecture
d. Whitehead conjecture

11. In mathematics, a _____ is a natural number which has exactly two distinct natural number divisors: 1 and itself. An infinitude of _____s exists, as demonstrated by Euclid around 300 BC. The first twenty-five _____s are:

2, 3, 5, 7, 11, 13, 17, 19, 23, 29, 31, 37, 41, 43, 47, 53, 59, 61, 67, 71, 73, 79, 83, 89, 97.

a. Highly composite number
c. Pronic number
b. Prime number
d. Perrin number

12. The word _____ has many distinct meanings in different fields of knowledge, depending on their methodologies and the context of discussion. Broadly speaking we can say that a _____ is some kind of belief or claim that (supposedly) explains, asserts, or consolidates some class of claims. Additionally, in contrast with a theorem the statement of the _____ is generally accepted only in some tentative fashion as opposed to regarding it as having been conclusively established.

a. Per mil
b. Defined
c. Transport of structure
d. Theory

13. In number theory, the _____ states that every natural number greater than 1 can be written as a unique product of prime numbers. For instance,

$$6936 = 2^3 \times 3 \times 17^2,$$

$$1200 = 2^4 \times 3 \times 5^2.$$

There are no other possible factorizations of 6936 or 1200 into non-negative prime numbers. The above representation collapses repeated prime factors into powers for easier identification.

    a. Feit–Thompson theorem
    b. Cyclic number
    c. Dedekind sums
    d. Fundamental theorem of arithmetic

14. _____, as that term is used in this article, is the mathematics written in Greek, developed from the 6th century BC to the 5th century AD around the Eastern shores of the Mediterranean. The word 'mathematics' itself derives from the ancient Greek μάθημα, meaning 'subject of instruction'.. The study of mathematics for its own sake and the use of generalized mathematical theories and proofs is the key difference between _____ and those of preceding civilizations.

    a. 2-3 heap
    b. Greek mathematics
    c. 1-center problem
    d. 120-cell

15. In mathematics, a _____ is a statement that can be proved on the basis of explicitly stated or previously agreed assumptions.

    a. Logical value
    b. Theorem
    c. Boolean function
    d. Disjunction introduction

16. In set theory, a _____ is a partially ordered set such that for each t ∈ T, the set {s ∈ T : s < t} is well-ordered by the relation <. For each t ∈ T, the order type of {s ∈ T : s < t} is called the height of t. The height of T itself is the least ordinal greater than the height of each element of T.

    a. Definable numbers
    b. Transitive reduction
    c. Set-theoretic topology
    d. Tree

17. In mathematics, a _____ is a convincing demonstration that some mathematical statement is necessarily true. _____s are obtained from deductive reasoning, rather than from inductive or empirical arguments. That is, a _____ must demonstrate that a statement is true in all cases, without a single exception.

    a. Proof
    b. Congruent
    c. Germ
    d. Conchoid

18. _____ reductio ad impossibile is a type of logical argument where one assumes a claim for the sake of argument and derives an absurd or ridiculous outcome, and then concludes that the original claim must have been wrong as it led to an absurd result.

Chapter 5. Number Theory

It makes use of the law of non-contradiction -- a statement cannot be both true and false. In some cases it may also make use of the law of excluded middle -- a statement must be either true or false.

- a. 120-cell
- b. 2-3 heap
- c. Reductio ad absurdum
- d. 1-center problem

19. In mathematics and physics, there are a _____ number of topics named in honor of Leonhard Euler . As well, many of these topics include their own unique function, equation, formula, identity, number, or other mathematical entity. Unfortunately however, many of these entities have been given simple names like Euler's function, Euler's equation, and Euler's formula, which are further confused by variations of the 'Euler'-prefix Overall though, Euler's work touched upon so many fields that he is often the earliest written reference on a given matter.
- a. List of trigonometry topics
- b. List of mathematical knots and links
- c. List of integrals of logarithmic functions
- d. Large

20. In mathematics, a _____ is a positive integer of the form

$$F_n = 2^{2^n} + 1$$

where n is a nonnegative integer. The first nine _____ s are (sequence A000215 in OEIS):

As of 2008, only F_0 to F_{11} have been completely factored.

If $2^n + 1$ is prime, and n > 0, it can be shown that n must be a power of two.

- a. Cabtaxi number
- b. Fermat number
- c. Q-Vandermonde identity
- d. Multiplicative number theory

21. _____ IPA: [pjÉ›Ê Ê dÉ™fÉ›Ê 'ma] (17 August 1601 or 1607/8 - 12 January 1665) was a French lawyer at the Parlement of Toulouse, France, and a mathematician who is given credit for early developments that led to modern calculus. In particular, he is recognized for his discovery of an original method of finding the greatest and the smallest ordinates of curved lines, which is analogous to that of the then unknown differential calculus, as well as his research into the theory of numbers. He also made notable contributions to analytic geometry, probability, and optics.
- a. Nikita Borisov
- b. Philip J. Davis
- c. Felix Hausdorff
- d. Pierre de Fermat

22. The _____ is a collaborative project of volunteers who use Prime95 and MPrime computer software that can be downloaded from the Internet for free in order to search for Mersenne prime numbers. The project was founded and the prime testing software was written by George Woltman. Scott Kurowski wrote the PrimeNet server that supports the research to demonstrate Entropia-distributed computing software, a company he founded in 1997.
- a. 120-cell
- b. 1-center problem
- c. Seventeen or Bust
- d. Great Internet Mersenne Prime Search

23. In mathematics, a Mersenne number is a positive integer that is one less than a power of two:

$$M_n = 2^n - 1.$$

Some definitions of Mersenne numbers require that the exponent n be prime.

A _____ is a Mersenne number that is prime. As of October 2008, only 46 _____ s are known; the largest known prime number ($2^{43,112,609} - 1$) is a _____, and in modern times, the largest known prime has almost always been a _____.

- a. 1-center problem
- b. Mersenne Prime
- c. Mersenne number
- d. Red-black tree

24. In mathematics, a _____ is a positive integer that is one less than a power of two:

$$M_n = 2^n - 1.$$

Some definitions of _____ s require that the exponent n be prime.

A Mersenne prime is a _____ that is prime. As of October 2008, only 46 Mersenne primes are known; the largest known prime number ($2^{43,112,609} - 1$) is a Mersenne prime, and in modern times, the largest known prime has almost always been a Mersenne prime.

- a. Mersenne number
- b. 1-center problem
- c. Mersenne prime
- d. Red-black tree

25. _____ (Electron Mechanics) refers to the flow of charge (moving electrons) through nonmetal conductors (mainly semiconductors), whereas electrical refers to the flow of charge through metal conductors. For example, flow of charge through silicon, which is not a metal, would come under _____; whereas flow of charge through copper, which is a metal, would come under electrical. This distinction started around 1906 with the invention by Lee De Forest of the triode.

- a. A posteriori
- b. A chemical equation
- c. A Mathematical Theory of Communication
- d. Electronics

26. In mathematics, a _____ is an expression constructed from variables and constants, using the operations of addition, subtraction, multiplication, and constant non-negative whole number exponents. For example, $x^2 - 4x + 7$ is a _____, but $x^2 - 4/x + 7x^{3/2}$ is not, because its second term involves division by the variable x and also because its third term contains an exponent that is not a whole number.

_____ s are one of the most important concepts in algebra and throughout mathematics and science.

- a. Coimage
- b. Polynomial
- c. Semifield
- d. Group extension

27. In mathematics and in the sciences, a _____ (plural: _____ e, formulæ or _____ s) is a concise way of expressing information symbolically (as in a mathematical or chemical _____), or a general relationship between quantities. One of many famous _____ e is Albert Einstein's $E = mc^2$ (see special relativity

Chapter 5. Number Theory

In mathematics, a _____ is a key to solve an equation with variables. For example, the problem of determining the volume of a sphere is one that requires a significant amount of integral calculus to solve.

- a. 2-3 heap
- b. 120-cell
- c. 1-center problem
- d. Formula

28. In mathematics, in the realm of group theory, a group is said to be _____ if it equals its own commutator subgroup if the group has no nontrivial abelian quotients.

The smallest _____ group is the alternating group A_5. More generally, any non-abelian simple group is _____ since the commutator subgroup is a normal subgroup with abelian quotient.

- a. Group of Lie type
- b. Perfect
- c. Quaternion group
- d. Free product

29. In mathematics, a _____ is defined as a positive integer which is the sum of its proper positive divisors, that is, the sum of the positive divisors excluding the number itself. Equivalently, a _____ is a number that is half the sum of all of its positive divisors, or = 2n.

The first _____ is 6, because 1, 2, and 3 are its proper positive divisors, and 1 + 2 + 3 = 6.

- a. Perfect number
- b. Nonhypotenuse number
- c. Blum integer
- d. Leonardo numbers

30. In mathematics, an _____ or excessive number is a number n for which σσ− 2n is called the abundance of n.
- a. Abundant number
- b. Unitary perfect number
- c. Integer sequence
- d. Idoneal number

31. _____ are two different numbers so related that the sum of the proper divisors of one of the numbers is equal to the other, one being considered as a proper divisor but not the number itself. Such a pair is; for the proper divisors of 220 are 1, 2, 4, 5, 10, 11, 20, 22, 44, 55 and 110, of which the sum is 284; and the proper divisors of 284 are 1, 2, 4, 71, and 142, of which the sum is 220. _____ were known to the Pythagoreans, who credited them with many mystical properties.
- a. Auxiliary functions
- b. Arithmetic derivative
- c. Amicable numbers
- d. Automorphic form

32. In mathematics, a _____ or defective number is a number n for which σσ
- a. Highly totient number
- b. Woodall number
- c. Kynea number
- d. Deficient number

33. In number theory, a _____ is a natural number that shares a certain characteristic called abundancy, the ratio between the sum of divisors of the number and the number itself, with one or more other numbers. Two numbers with the same abundancy form a friendly pair. Larger clubs of mutually _____s also exist.

a. Perfect power
c. Friendly number
b. Class number formula
d. Quote notation

34. A _____ is the transfer of an interest in property (or in law the equivalent - a charge) to a lender as a security for a debt - usually a loan of money. While a _____ in itself is not a debt, it is lender's security for a debt. It is a transfer of an interest in land (or the equivalent), from the owner to the _____ lender, on the condition that this interest will be returned to the owner of the real estate when the terms of the _____ have been satisfied or performed.
   a. 1-center problem
   c. 120-cell
   b. 2-3 heap
   d. Mortgage

35. In mathematics, a _____ is a natural number that is abundant but not semiperfect. In other words, the sum of the proper divisors of the number is greater than the number, but no subset of those divisors sums to the number itself.

The smallest _____ is 70.

   a. Regular paperfolding sequence
   c. Hofstadter sequence
   b. Carol number
   d. Weird number

36. The _____ has two similar but distinct meanings. The name is attributed to Harvey Dubner and is a portmanteau of prime and factorial. The _____ $p_n\#$ is defined as the product of the first n primes:

$$p_n\# = \prod_{k=1}^{n} p_k$$

where p_k is the kth prime number.

   a. Multiply perfect number
   c. Super-Poulet number
   b. Perfect number
   d. Primorial

37. In mathematics, the _____ or Pythagoras' theorem is a relation in Euclidean geometry among the three sides of a right triangle. The theorem is named after the Greek mathematician Pythagoras, who by tradition is credited with its discovery and proof, although it is often argued that knowledge of the theory predates him.. The theorem is as follows:

In any right triangle, the area of the square whose side is the hypotenuse is equal to the sum of the areas of the squares whose sides are the two legs.

   a. 120-cell
   c. 2-3 heap
   b. Pythagorean theorem
   d. 1-center problem

38. A _____ is a software program that facilitates symbolic mathematics. The core functionality of a CAS is manipulation of mathematical expressions in symbolic form.

Chapter 5. Number Theory

The symbolic manipulations supported typically include

- simplification to the smallest possible expression or some standard form, including automatic simplification with assumptions and simplification with constraints
- substitution of symbolic, functors or numeric values for expressions
- change of form of expressions: expanding products and powers, partial and full factorization, rewriting as partial fractions, constraint satisfaction, rewriting trigonometric functions as exponentials, etc.
- partial and total differentiation
- symbolic constrained and unconstrained global optimization
- solution of linear and some non-linear equations over various domains
- solution of some differential and difference equations
- taking some limits
- some indefinite and definite integration, including multidimensional integrals
- integral transforms
- arbitrary-precision numeric operations
- Series operations such as expansion, summation and products
- matrix operations including products, inverses, etc.
- display of mathematical expressions in two-dimensional mathematical form, often using typesetting systems similar to TeX
- add-ons for use in applied mathematics such as physics packages for physical computation
- plotting graphs and parametric plots of functions in two and three dimensions, and animating them
- APIs for linking it on an external program such as a database, or using in a programming language to use the _____
- drawing charts and diagrams
- string manipulation such as matching and searching
- statistical computation
- Theorem proving and verification
- graphic production and editing such as CGI and signal processing as image processing
- sound synthesis

Many also include a programming language, allowing users to implement their own algorithms.

Some _____s focus on a specific area of application; these are typically developed in academia and are free.

a. 1-center problem
c. 120-cell

b. 2-3 heap
d. Computer algebra system

39. A _____ is a book of alphabetically listed words in a specific language, with definitions, etymologies, pronunciations, and other information; or a book of alphabetically listed words in one language with their PIE equivalents in another, also known as a lexicon.

In many languages, words can appear in many different forms, but only the undeclined or unconjugated form appears as the headword in most dictionaries. Dictionaries are most commonly found in the form of a book, but some newer dictionaries, like StarDict and the New Oxford American _____ are _____ software running on PDAs or computers.

a. 120-cell
b. 1-center problem
c. 2-3 heap
d. Dictionary

40. In number theory, the _____ is an algorithm to determine the greatest common divisor of two elements of any Euclidean domain. Its major significance is that it does not require factoring the two integers, and it is also significant in that it is one of the oldest algorithms known, dating back to the ancient Greeks.

The _____ is one of the oldest algorithms known, since it appeared in Euclid's Elements around 300 BC.

a. A posteriori
b. A chemical equation
c. Euclidean algorithm
d. A Mathematical Theory of Communication

41. In mathematics, computing, linguistics and related subjects, an _____ is a sequence of finite instructions, often used for calculation and data processing. It is formally a type of effective method in which a list of well-defined instructions for completing a task will, when given an initial state, proceed through a well-defined series of successive states, eventually terminating in an end-state. The transition from one state to the next is not necessarily deterministic; some _____s, known as probabilistic _____s, incorporate randomness.

a. Approximate counting algorithm
b. Out-of-core
c. In-place algorithm
d. Algorithm

42. In arithmetic and number theory, the _____ or lowest common multiple or smallest common multiple of two integers a and b is the smallest positive integer that is a multiple of both a and b. Since it is a multiple, it can be divided by a and b without a remainder. If either a or b is 0, so that there is no such positive integer, then lc is defined to be zero.

a. Lowest common denominator
b. Plus-minus sign
c. Plus and minus signs
d. Least common multiple

43. In mathematics, _____ is a property that a binary operation can have. It means that, within an expression containing two or more of the same associative operators in a row, the order that the operations are performed does not matter as long as the sequence of the operands is not changed. That is, rearranging the parentheses in such an expression will not change its value.

a. Associativity
b. Idempotence
c. Unital
d. Algebraically closed

44. _____ is the mathematical operation of scaling one number by another. It is one of the four basic operations in elementary arithmetic.

Chapter 5. Number Theory

_____ is defined for whole numbers in terms of repeated addition; for example, 4 multiplied by 3 can be calculated by adding 3 copies of 4 together:

$$4 + 4 + 4 = 12.$$

_____ of rational numbers and real numbers is defined by systematic generalization of this basic idea.

    a. Least common multiple
    b. Highest common factor
    c. Multiplication
    d. The number 0 is even.

45. In mathematics, the _____ of a number n is the number that, when added to n, yields zero. The _____ of n is denoted −n. For example, 7 is −7, because 7 + (−7) = 0, and the _____ of −0.3 is 0.3, because −0.3 + 0.3 = 0.
    a. Additive inverse
    b. Algebraic structure
    c. Arity
    d. Associativity

46. _____ is the likelihood or chance that something is the case or will happen. Theoretical _____ is used extensively in areas such as statistics, mathematics, science and philosophy to draw conclusions about the likelihood of potential events and the underlying mechanics of complex systems.

The word _____ does not have a consistent direct definition.

    a. Discrete random variable
    b. Standardized moment
    c. Statistical significance
    d. Probability

47. _____ is an abbreviation for Cryptographic Hardware and Embedded Systems, a workshop for cryptography research, focusing on hardware-related topics. _____ is a workshop sponsored by the International Association for Cryptologic Research. _____ was first held in Worcester, Massachusetts in 1999 at Worcester Polytechnic Institute.
    a. HC-256
    b. NLFSR
    c. Zimmermann-Sassaman key-signing protocol
    d. Ches

48. In mathematics, a function f is _____ of a function g if f whenever A and B are complementary angles. This definition typically applies to trigonometric functions.
    a. Birkhoff interpolation
    b. Balian-Low theorem
    c. Boxcar function
    d. Cofunction

49. In complex analysis, the _____ is a complex number which describes the behavior of line integrals of a meromorphic function around a singularity. _____s can be computed quite easily and, once known, allow the determination of more complicated path integrals via the _____ theorem.

The _____ of a meromorphic function f at an isolated singularity a, often denoted Res is the unique value R such that $f(z) - \dfrac{R}{(z-a)}$ has an analytic antiderivative in a punctured disk $0 < |z - a| < \delta$.

a. Functional
c. Block size

b. Residue
d. Function

50. Leonardo of Pisa (c. 1170 - c. 1250), also known as Leonardo Pisano, Leonardo Bonacci, Leonardo _____, or, most commonly, simply _____, was an Italian mathematician, considered by some 'the most talented mathematician of the Middle Ages'.

a. Guido Castelnuovo
c. Fibonacci

b. Ralph C. Merkle
d. Harry Hinsley

51. In statistics, an _____ comes from two variables that are related and is often confused with causality though _____ does not imply a causal relationship. In formal statistics, correlation and _____ are related but not entirely overlapping concepts.

For example, the United Nations studied governmental failure--when governments fall or are overthrown and found that the best indicator of a government about to fall was the infant mortality rate.

a. Integration
c. Efficiency

b. Outcome
d. Association

52. The _____ is a group that promotes research into mathematics related to the Fibonacci numbers. The association was founded in 1963 by the American mathematician Verner E. Hoggatt Jr. and brother Alfred Brousseau at the University of Santa Clara, California.

a. 1-center problem
c. Lucas pseudoprime

b. Fibonacci Association
d. Pisano period

53. A _____, from the French patron, is a type of theme of recurring events of or objects, sometimes referred to as elements of a set. These elements repeat in a predictable manner. It can be a template or model which can be used to generate things or parts of a thing, especially if the things that are created have enough in common for the underlying _____ to be inferred, in which case the things are said to exhibit the unique _____.

a. 1-center problem
c. 2-3 heap

b. 120-cell
d. Pattern

54. In mathematics and the arts, two quantities are in the _____ if the ratio between the sum of those quantities and the larger one is the same as the ratio between the larger one and the smaller. The _____ is an irrational mathematical constant, approximately 1.6180339887.

At least since the Renaissance, many artists and architects have proportioned their works to approximate the _____--especially in the form of the golden rectangle, in which the ratio of the longer side to the shorter is the _____--believing this proportion to be aesthetically pleasing.

a. 120-cell
c. 2-3 heap

b. 1-center problem
d. Golden ratio

55. In mathematics, a _____ is a particular generalisation of the Fibonacci numbers and Lucas numbers. _____s are named after French mathematician Edouard Lucas.

Chapter 5. Number Theory

Given two integer parameters P and Q which satisfy

$$P^2 - 4Q \neq 0$$

the _____s of the first kind U_nn

$$U_0(P,Q) = 0$$
$$U_1(P,Q) = 1$$

and

$$V_0(P,Q) = 2$$
$$V_1(P,Q) = P$$

The characteristic equation of _____s is:

$$x^2 - Px + Q = 0$$

It has the discriminant D = P² − 4Q and the roots:

$$a = \frac{P + \sqrt{D}}{2} \quad \text{and} \quad b = \frac{P - \sqrt{D}}{2}.$$

Note that a and b are distinct because $D \neq 0.$

The terms of _____s can be defined in terms of a and b as follows

$$U_n(P,Q) = \frac{a^n - b^n}{a - b} = \frac{a^n - b^n}{\sqrt{D}}$$

$$V_n(P,Q) = a^n + b^n$$

from which one can derive the relations

$$a^n = \frac{V_n + U_n\sqrt{D}}{2}$$

$$b^n = \frac{V_n - U_n\sqrt{D}}{2}$$

a. 2-3 heap
c. 1-center problem
b. 120-cell
d. Lucas sequence

56. A _____ is one of the basic shapes of geometry: a polygon with three corners or vertices and three sides or edges which are line segments. A _____ with vertices A, B, and C is denoted ABC.

In Euclidean geometry any three non-collinear points determine a unique _____ and a unique plane.

a. Kepler triangle
c. 1-center problem
b. Triangle
d. Fuhrmann circle

57. In World War II, _____ was the United States codename for intelligence derived from the cryptanalysis of PURPLE, a Japanese foreign office cipher.

The Japanese and the Germans both used the Enigma machine to encode their cable traffic. The Japanese Enigma-based system was called PURPLE by U.S. cryptographers.

a. Bandwidth
c. Magic
b. Discontinuity
d. Basis

58. In recreational mathematics, a _____ of order n is an arrangement of n^2 numbers, usually distinct integers, in a square, such that the n numbers in all rows, all columns, and both diagonals sum to the same constant. A normal _____ contains the integers from 1 to n^2. The term '_____' is also sometimes used to refer to any of various types of word square.

a. 1-center problem
c. 120-cell
b. Prime reciprocal magic square
d. Magic square

59. In mathematics, an _____ in the sense of ring theory is a subring $\mathcal{O}$ of a ring R that satisfies the conditions

1. R is a ring which is a finite-dimensional algebra over the rational number field $\mathbb{Q}$
2. $\mathcal{O}$ spans R over $\mathbb{Q}$, so that $\mathbb{Q}\mathcal{O} = R$, and
3. $\mathcal{O}$ is a lattice in R.

The third condition can be stated more accurately, in terms of the extension of scalars of R to the real numbers, embedding R in a real vector space. In less formal terms, additively $\mathcal{O}$ should be a free abelian group generated by a basis for R over $\mathbb{Q}$.

The leading example is the case where R is a number field K and $\mathcal{O}$ is its ring of integers. In algebraic number theory there are examples for any K other than the rational field of proper subrings of the ring of integers that are also _____s.

a. Annihilator
b. Order
c. Algebraic
d. Efficiency

Chapter 6. The Real Numbers and Their Representations

1. In mathematics, the _____s may be described informally in several different ways. The _____s include both rational numbers, such as 42 and −23/129, and irrational numbers, such as pi and the square root of two; or, a _____ can be given by an infinite decimal representation, such as 2.4871773339...., where the digits continue in some way; or, the _____s may be thought of as points on an infinitely long number line.

These descriptions of the _____s, while intuitively accessible, are not sufficiently rigorous for the purposes of pure mathematics.

   a. Minkowski distance
   c. Real number
   b. Tally marks
   d. Pre-algebra

2. In mathematics, the _____ of a real number is its numerical value without regard to its sign. So, for example, 3 is the _____ of both 3 and −3.

The _____ of a number a is denoted by $|a|$.

Generalizations of the _____ for real numbers occur in a wide variety of mathematical settings.

   a. A chemical equation
   c. Area hyperbolic functions
   b. A Mathematical Theory of Communication
   d. Absolute value

3. _____ refers to any mathematics of the peoples of Mesopotamia, from the days of the early Sumerians to the fall of Babylon in 539 BC. In contrast to the scarcity of sources in Egyptian mathematics, our knowledge of _____ is derived from some 400 clay tablets unearthed since the 1850s. Written in Cuneiform script, tablets were inscribed while the clay was moist, and baked hard in an oven or by the heat of the sun.
   a. 2-3 heap
   c. 1-center problem
   b. 120-cell
   d. Babylonian mathematics

4. In mathematics, a _____ can mean either an element of the set {1, 2, 3, ...} or an element of the set {0, 1, 2, 3, ...}. The latter is especially preferred in mathematical logic, set theory, and computer science.

_____s have two main purposes: they can be used for counting, and they can be used for ordering.

   a. Suslin cardinal
   c. Strong partition cardinal
   b. Cardinal numbers
   d. Natural number

5. _____, as that term is used in this article, is the mathematics written in Greek, developed from the 6th century BC to the 5th century AD around the Eastern shores of the Mediterranean. The word 'mathematics' itself derives from the ancient Greek μαθημα, meaning 'subject of instruction'.. The study of mathematics for its own sake and the use of generalized mathematical theories and proofs is the key difference between _____ and those of preceding civilizations.
   a. 120-cell
   c. Greek mathematics
   b. 2-3 heap
   d. 1-center problem

6. In mathematics, a _____ can mean either an element of the set {1, 2, 3, ...} (i.e the positive integers) or an element of the set {0, 1, 2, 3, ...} (i.e. the non-negative integers).

a. Bounded
c. FISH
b. Degrees of freedom
d. Whole number

7. A _____ is a software program that facilitates symbolic mathematics. The core functionality of a CAS is manipulation of mathematical expressions in symbolic form.

The symbolic manipulations supported typically include

- simplification to the smallest possible expression or some standard form, including automatic simplification with assumptions and simplification with constraints
- substitution of symbolic, functors or numeric values for expressions
- change of form of expressions: expanding products and powers, partial and full factorization, rewriting as partial fractions, constraint satisfaction, rewriting trigonometric functions as exponentials, etc.
- partial and total differentiation
- symbolic constrained and unconstrained global optimization
- solution of linear and some non-linear equations over various domains
- solution of some differential and difference equations
- taking some limits
- some indefinite and definite integration, including multidimensional integrals
- integral transforms
- arbitrary-precision numeric operations
- Series operations such as expansion, summation and products
- matrix operations including products, inverses, etc.
- display of mathematical expressions in two-dimensional mathematical form, often using typesetting systems similar to TeX
- add-ons for use in applied mathematics such as physics packages for physical computation
- plotting graphs and parametric plots of functions in two and three dimensions, and animating them
- APIs for linking it on an external program such as a database, or using in a programming language to use the _____
- drawing charts and diagrams
- string manipulation such as matching and searching
- statistical computation
- Theorem proving and verification
- graphic production and editing such as CGI and signal processing as image processing
- sound synthesis

Many also include a programming language, allowing users to implement their own algorithms.

Some _____s focus on a specific area of application; these are typically developed in academia and are free.

a. 120-cell
c. 2-3 heap
b. 1-center problem
d. Computer algebra system

8. _____ is the title of a short book on logic by Gottlob Frege, published in 1879, and is also the name of the formal system set out in that book.

_____ is usually translated as concept writing or concept notation; the full title of the book identifies it as 'a formula language, modelled on that of arithmetic, of pure thought.' The _____ was arguably the most important publication in logic since Aristotle founded the subject. Frege's motivation for developing his formal approach to logic resembled Leibniz's motivation for his calculus ratiocinator.

    a. Begriffsschrift   b. 1-center problem
    c. 2-3 heap   d. 120-cell

9. In mathematics, the _____ of a Euclidean space is a special point, usually denoted by the letter O, used as a fixed point of reference for the geometry of the surrounding space. In a Cartesian coordinate system, the _____ is the point where the axes of the system intersect. In Euclidean geometry, the _____ may be chosen freely as any convenient point of reference.

    a. Autonomous system   b. OMAC
    c. Interval   d. Origin

10. The _____ are the set of numbers consisting of the natural numbers including 0 and their negatives. They are numbers that can be written without a fractional or decimal component, and fall within the set {... −2, −1, 0, 1, 2, ...}.

    a. A Mathematical Theory of Communication   b. A chemical equation
    c. A posteriori   d. Integers

11. In mathematics, a _____ is a number which can be expressed as a ratio of two integers. Non-integer _____s are usually written as the vulgar fraction $\frac{a}{b}$, where b is not zero. a is called the numerator, and b the denominator.

    a. Rational number   b. Tally marks
    c. Pre-algebra   d. Minkowski distance

12. A _____ of a non-negative real number r is an expression of the form

$$r = \sum_{i=0}^{\infty} \frac{a_i}{10^i}$$

where a_0 is a nonnegative integer, and $a_1, a_2, \ldots$ are integers satisfying $0 \leq a_i \leq 9$; this is often written more briefly as

$$r = a_0.a_1 a_2 a_3 \ldots.$$

That is to say, a_0 is the integer part of r, not necessarily between 0 and 9, and $a_1, a_2, a_3, \ldots$ are the digits forming the fractional part of r.

Chapter 6. The Real Numbers and Their Representations

Any real number can be approximated to any desired degree of accuracy by rational numbers with finite _____s.

Assume $x \geq 0$. Then for every integer $n \geq 1$ there is a finite decimal $r_n = a_0.a_1 a_2 \cdots a_n$ such that

$$r_n \leq x < r_n + \frac{1}{10^n}.$$

Proof:

Let $r_n = \frac{p}{10^n}$, where $p = \lfloor 10^n x \rfloor$.

a. 1-center problem
b. 120-cell
c. 2-3 heap
d. Decimal representation

13. In mathematics, hyperbolic n-space, denoted H^n, is the maximally symmetric, simply connected, n-dimensional Riemannian manifold with constant sectional curvature −1. _____ is the principal example of a space exhibiting hyperbolic geometry. It can be thought of as the negative-curvature analogue of the n-sphere.
    a. Margulis lemma
    b. Horocycle
    c. Hyperbolic space
    d. Hyperbolic geometry

14. In mathematics, an _____ in the sense of ring theory is a subring $\mathcal{O}$ of a ring R that satisfies the conditions

    1. R is a ring which is a finite-dimensional algebra over the rational number field $\mathbb{Q}$
    2. $\mathcal{O}$ spans R over $\mathbb{Q}$, so that $\mathbb{Q}\mathcal{O} = R$, and
    3. $\mathcal{O}$ is a lattice in R.

The third condition can be stated more accurately, in terms of the extension of scalars of R to the real numbers, embedding R in a real vector space. In less formal terms, additively $\mathcal{O}$ should be a free abelian group generated by a basis for R over $\mathbb{Q}$.

The leading example is the case where R is a number field K and $\mathcal{O}$ is its ring of integers. In algebraic number theory there are examples for any K other than the rational field of proper subrings of the ring of integers that are also _____s.

a. Order
b. Efficiency
c. Algebraic
d. Annihilator

15. In mathematics, an inequality is a statement about the relative size or order of two objects. For example 14 > 10, or 14 is _____ 10. The notation a > b means that a is _____ b and 'a' would be to the right of 'b' on a number line.
    a. Cauchy-Schwarz inequality
    b. Minkowski inequality
    c. Greater than
    d. FKG inequality

Chapter 6. The Real Numbers and Their Representations

16. _____ is the mathematical operation of scaling one number by another. It is one of the four basic operations in elementary arithmetic.

_____ is defined for whole numbers in terms of repeated addition; for example, 4 multiplied by 3 can be calculated by adding 3 copies of 4 together:

$$4 + 4 + 4 = 12.$$

_____ of rational numbers and real numbers is defined by systematic generalization of this basic idea.

   a. Highest common factor
   b. Multiplication
   c. Least common multiple
   d. The number 0 is even.

17. In mathematics, the _____ of a number n is the number that, when added to n, yields zero. The _____ of n is denoted −n. For example, 7 is −7, because 7 + (−7) = 0, and the _____ of −0.3 is 0.3, because −0.3 + 0.3 = 0.
   a. Associativity
   b. Algebraic structure
   c. Arity
   d. Additive inverse

18. In mathematics, a _____ for a number x, denoted by $\frac{1}{x}$ or x^{-1}, is a number which when multiplied by x yields the multiplicative identity, 1. The _____ of x is also called the reciprocal of x. The _____ of a fraction p/q is q/p.
   a. Golden function
   b. Multiplicative inverse
   c. Hyperbolic function
   d. Double exponential

19. In mathematics, the multiplicative inverse of a number x, denoted 1/x or x^{-1}, is the number which, when multiplied by x, yields 1. The multiplicative inverse of x is also called the _____ of x.
   a. 2-3 heap
   b. 1-center problem
   c. 120-cell
   d. Reciprocal

20. _____ is the likelihood or chance that something is the case or will happen. Theoretical _____ is used extensively in areas such as statistics, mathematics, science and philosophy to draw conclusions about the likelihood of potential events and the underlying mechanics of complex systems.

The word _____ does not have a consistent direct definition.

   a. Probability
   b. Standardized moment
   c. Discrete random variable
   d. Statistical significance

21. Leonardo of Pisa (c. 1170 - c. 1250), also known as Leonardo Pisano, Leonardo Bonacci, Leonardo _____, or, most commonly, simply _____, was an Italian mathematician, considered by some 'the most talented mathematician of the Middle Ages'.
   a. Guido Castelnuovo
   b. Harry Hinsley
   c. Fibonacci
   d. Ralph C. Merkle

Chapter 6. The Real Numbers and Their Representations

22. In cryptography, the _____ was a method devised by Polish mathematician-cryptologist Jerzy Różycki, at the Polish General Staff's Cipher Bureau, to facilitate decrypting German Enigma messages. This method sometimes made it possible to determine which of the Enigma machine's rotors was at the far right, that is, in the position where the rotor always revolved at every depression of a key.

- Biuro Szyfrów

   a. TWIRL   b. FROSTBURG
   c. Bombe   d. Clock

23. In mathematics, _____ is a system of arithmetic for integers, where numbers 'wrap around' after they reach a certain value -- the modulus. _____ was introduced by Carl Friedrich Gauss in his book Disquisitiones Arithmeticae, published in 1801.

A familiar use of _____ is its use in the 24-hour clock: the arithmetic of time-keeping in which the day runs from midnight to midnight and is divided into 24 hours, numbered from 0 to 23.

   a. Modular arithmetic   b. Discrete logarithm
   c. Multiplicative group of integers modulo n   d. Residue number system

24. In mathematics, a _____ is the end result of a division problem. It can also be expressed as the number of times the divisor divides into the dividend.
   a. Marginal cost   b. Quotient
   c. Notation   d. Limiting

25. In algebra and computer programming, when a number or expression is both preceded and followed by a binary operation, a rule is required for which operation should be applied first; this rule is known as an _____ . From the earliest use of mathematical notation, multiplication took precedence over addition, whichever side of a number it appeared on. Thus 3 + 4 × 5 = 5 × 4 + 3 = 23.
   a. Order of Operations   b. Isomorphism class
   c. Identity element   d. Algebraic K-theory

26. In mathematics, _____ is a property that a binary operation can have. It means that, within an expression containing two or more of the same associative operators in a row, the order that the operations are performed does not matter as long as the sequence of the operands is not changed. That is, rearranging the parentheses in such an expression will not change its value.
   a. Algebraically closed   b. Associativity
   c. Unital   d. Idempotence

27. In mathematics, and in particular in abstract algebra, distributivity is a property of binary operations that generalises the _____ law from elementary algebra.
   a. Closure with a twist   b. Permutation
   c. General linear group   d. Distributive

Chapter 6. The Real Numbers and Their Representations

28. In mathematics, the term _____ has several different important meanings:

- An _____ is an equality that remains true regardless of the values of any variables that appear within it, to distinguish it from an equality which is true under more particular conditions. For this, the 'triple bar' symbol ≡ is sometimes used.
- In algebra, an _____ or _____ element of a set S with a binary operation Â· is an element e that, when combined with any element x of S, produces that same x. That is, eÂ·x = xÂ·e = x for all x in S.
    - The _____ function from a set S to itself, often denoted id or id$_S$, s the function such that i = x for all x in S. This function serves as the _____ element in the set of all functions from S to itself with respect to function composition.
    - In linear algebra, the _____ matrix of size n is the n-by-n square matrix with ones on the main diagonal and zeros elsewhere. This matrix serves as the _____ with respect to matrix multiplication.

A common example of the first meaning is the trigonometric _____

$$\sin^2 \theta + \cos^2 \theta = 1$$

which is true for all real values of θ, as opposed to

$$\cos \theta = 1,$$

which is true only for some values of θ, not all. For example, the latter equation is true when $\theta = 0$, false when $\theta = 2$

The concepts of 'additive _____' and 'multiplicative _____' are central to the Peano axioms. The number 0 is the 'additive _____' for integers, real numbers, and complex numbers. For the real numbers, for all $a \in \mathbb{R}$,

$$0 + a = a,$$

$$a + 0 = a, \text{ and}$$

$$0 + 0 = 0.$$

Similarly, The number 1 is the 'multiplicative _____' for integers, real numbers, and complex numbers.

a. Action
c. ARIA
b. Intersection
d. Identity

29. In mathematics, an _____ is a special type of element of a set with respect to a binary operation on that set. It leaves other elements unchanged when combined with them. This is used for groups and related concepts.
a. Algebraically closed
c. Universal algebra
b. Arity
d. Identity element

Chapter 6. The Real Numbers and Their Representations

30. In mathematics, an _____ or member of a set is any one of the distinct objects that make up that set.

Writing A = {1,2,3,4}, means that the _____s of the set A are the numbers 1, 2, 3 and 4. Groups of _____s of A, for example {1,2}, are subsets of A.

a. Ideal
c. Order
b. Universal code
d. Element

31. In mathematics, an _____, or central tendency of a data set refers to a measure of the 'middle' or 'expected' value of the data set. There are many different descriptive statistics that can be chosen as a measurement of the central tendency of the data items.

An _____ is a single value that is meant to typify a list of values.

a. A chemical equation
c. Average
b. A Mathematical Theory of Communication
d. A posteriori

32. In statistics, _____ has two related meanings:

- the arithmetic _____.
- the expected value of a random variable, which is also called the population _____.

It is sometimes stated that the '_____' _____s average. This is incorrect if '_____' is taken in the specific sense of 'arithmetic _____' as there are different types of averages: the _____, median, and mode. For instance, average house prices almost always use the median value for the average.

For a real-valued random variable X, the _____ is the expectation of X.

a. Mean
c. Statistical population
b. Proportional hazards model
d. Probability

33. The _____ of a material is defined as its mass per unit volume:

$$\rho = \frac{m}{V}$$

Different materials usually have different densities, so _____ is an important concept regarding buoyancy, metal purity and packaging.

In some cases _____ is expressed as the dimensionless quantities specific gravity or relative _____, in which case it is expressed in multiples of the _____ of some other standard material, usually water or air.

In a well-known story, Archimedes was given the task of determining whether King Hiero's goldsmith was embezzling gold during the manufacture of a wreath dedicated to the gods and replacing it with another, cheaper alloy.

a. 120-cell
b. Density
c. 1-center problem
d. 2-3 heap

34. A _____ typically refers to a class of handheld calculators that are capable of plotting graphs, solving simultaneous equations, and performing numerous other tasks with variables. Most popular _____s are also programmable, allowing the user to create customized programs, typically for scientific/engineering and education applications. Due to their large displays intended for graphing, they can also accommodate several lines of text and calculations at a time.
   a. Genus
   b. Bump mapping
   c. Support vector machines
   d. Graphing calculator

35. In mathematics, a _____ is a convincing demonstration that some mathematical statement is necessarily true. _____s are obtained from deductive reasoning, rather than from inductive or empirical arguments. That is, a _____ must demonstrate that a statement is true in all cases, without a single exception.
   a. Proof
   b. Germ
   c. Conchoid
   d. Congruent

36. _____ reductio ad impossibile is a type of logical argument where one assumes a claim for the sake of argument and derives an absurd or ridiculous outcome, and then concludes that the original claim must have been wrong as it led to an absurd result.

It makes use of the law of non-contradiction -- a statement cannot be both true and false. In some cases it may also make use of the law of excluded middle -- a statement must be either true or false.

   a. 2-3 heap
   b. 1-center problem
   c. 120-cell
   d. Reductio ad absurdum

37. A _____ is a device for performing mathematical calculations, distinguished from a computer by having a limited problem solving ability and an interface optimized for interactive calculation rather than programming. _____s can be hardware or software, and mechanical or electronic, and are often built into devices such as PDAs or mobile phones.

Modern electronic _____s are generally small, digital, and usually inexpensive.

   a. 2-3 heap
   b. 120-cell
   c. 1-center problem
   d. Calculator

38. The mathematical concept of a _____ expresses the intuitive idea of deterministic dependence between two quantities, one of which is viewed as primary and the other as secondary. A _____ then is a way to associate a unique output for each input of a specified type, for example, a real number or an element of a given set.
   a. Coherent
   b. Going up
   c. Function
   d. Grill

39. In vascular plants, the _____ is the organ of a plant body that typically lies below the surface of the soil. This is not always the case, however, since a _____ can also be aerial (that is, growing above the ground) or aerating (that is, growing up above the ground or especially above water.) Furthermore, a stem normally occurring below ground is not exceptional either

Chapter 6. The Real Numbers and Their Representations

    a. 1-center problem
    b. Root
    c. 2-3 heap
    d. 120-cell

40. In mathematics, a _____ of a number x is a number r such that r^2 = x, or, in other words, a number r whose square is x. Every non-negative real number x has a unique non-negative _____, called the principal _____, which is denoted with a radical symbol as $\sqrt{x}$, or, using exponent notation, as $x^{1/2}$. For example, the principal _____ of 9 is 3, denoted $\sqrt{9}$ = 3, because 3^2 = 3 × 3 = 9.
    a. Multiplicative inverse
    b. Hyperbolic functions
    c. Square root
    d. Double exponential

41. In mathematics, the _____ functions are functions of an angle; they are important when studying triangles and modeling periodic phenomena, among many other applications.
    a. Gudermannian function
    b. Law of sines
    c. Coversine
    d. Trigonometric

42. In mathematics, the _____ are functions of an angle. They are important in the study of triangles and modeling periodic phenomena, among many other applications. _____ are commonly defined as ratios of two sides of a right triangle containing the angle, and can equivalently be defined as the lengths of various line segments from a unit circle.
    a. Trigonometric functions
    b. Law of sines
    c. Trigonometric integrals
    d. Sine

43. _____ is a general term for any type of information processing. This includes phenomena ranging from human thinking to calculations with a more narrow meaning. _____ is a process following a well-defined model that is understood and can be expressed in an algorithm, protocol, network topology, etc.
    a. 2-3 heap
    b. 1-center problem
    c. 120-cell
    d. Computation

44. The _____ governs the differentiation of products of differentiable functions.
    a. 120-cell
    b. 1-center problem
    c. Reciprocal Rule
    d. Product rule

45. Exponentiation is a mathematical operation, written a^n, involving two numbers, the base a and the _____ n. When n is a positive integer, exponentiation corresponds to repeated multiplication:

$$a^n = \underbrace{a \times \cdots \times a}_{n},$$

just as multiplication by a positive integer corresponds to repeated addition:

$$a \times n = \underbrace{a + \cdots + a}_{n}.$$

The _____ is usually shown as a superscript to the right of the base. The exponentiation a^n can be read as: a raised to the n-th power, a raised to the power [of] n or possibly a raised to the _____ [of] n, or more briefly: a to the n-th power or a to the power [of] n, or even more briefly: a to the n.

a. Exponentiating by squaring
b. Exponential tree
c. Exponential sum
d. Exponent

46. In mathematics, an algebraic group G contains a unique maximal normal solvable subgroup; and this subgroup is closed. Its identity component is called the _____ of G.
   a. Radical
   b. Barycentric coordinates
   c. Block size
   d. Composite

47. In abstract algebra, a field extension L /K is called _____ if every element of L is _____ over K. Field extensions which are not _____.

For example, the field extension R/Q, that is the field of real numbers as an extension of the field of rational numbers, is transcendental, while the field extensions C/R and Q

   a. Identity
   b. Ideal
   c. Echo
   d. Algebraic

48. _____ involves reducing the number of significant digits in a number. The result of _____ is a 'shorter' number having fewer non-zero digits yet similar in magnitude. The result is less precise but easier to use.
   a. Hyper operator
   b. Sudan function
   c. Shabakh
   d. Rounding

49. In a positional numeral system, the decimal separator is a symbol used to mark the boundary between the integral and the fractional parts of a decimal numeral. When used in context of Arabic numerals, terms implying the symbol used are _____ and decimal comma.

The decimal separator is mathematically a radix point.

   a. Decimal point
   b. Tetradecimal
   c. Hexadecimal
   d. Fibonacci coding

50. _____ is the tendency of a force to rotate an object about some axis. Just as a force is a push or a pull, a _____ can be thought of as a twist. The symbol for _____ is τ, the Greek letter tau.
   a. 1-center problem
   b. Differential geometry of surfaces
   c. Torque
   d. Least significant bit

51. In chemistry, _____ is the measure of how much of a given substance there is mixed with another substance. This can apply to any sort of chemical mixture, but most frequently the concept is limited to homogeneous solutions, where it refers to the amount of solute in the solvent.

To concentrate a solution, one must add more solute, or reduce the amount of solvent (for instance, by selective evaporation.)

   a. Concentration
   b. 1-center problem
   c. 2-3 heap
   d. 120-cell

Chapter 6. The Real Numbers and Their Representations

52. In mathematics, the _____s are an extension of the real numbers obtained by adjoining an imaginary unit, denoted i, which satisfies:

$$i^2 = -1.$$

Every _____ can be written in the form a + bi, where a and b are real numbers called the real part and the imaginary part of the _____, respectively.

_____s are a field, and thus have addition, subtraction, multiplication, and division operations. These operations extend the corresponding operations on real numbers, although with a number of additional elegant and useful properties, e.g., negative real numbers can be obtained by squaring _____s.

 a. Real part
 b. 120-cell
 c. Complex number
 d. 1-center problem

53. _____ Galilei (15 February 1564 - 8 January 1642) was a Tuscan physicist, mathematician, astronomer, and philosopher who played a major role in the Scientific Revolution. His achievements include improvements to the telescope and consequent astronomical observations, and support for Copernicanism. _____ has been called the 'father of modern observational astronomy', the 'father of modern physics', the 'father of science', and 'the Father of Modern Science.' The motion of uniformly accelerated objects, taught in nearly all high school and introductory college physics courses, was studied by _____ as the subject of kinematics.

 a. David Naccache
 b. Jan Kowalewski
 c. Francesco Severi
 d. Galileo

54. In mathematics, an _____ is a complex number whose squared value is a real number less than or equal to zero. The imaginary unit, denoted by i or j, is an example of an _____. If y is a real number, then i·y is an _____, because:

$$(i \cdot y)^2 = i^2 \cdot y^2 = -y^2 \leq 0.$$

They were defined in 1572 by Rafael Bombelli.

 a. A Mathematical Theory of Communication
 b. A posteriori
 c. Imaginary number
 d. A chemical equation

55. In mathematics, the _____ of a complex number z, is the second element of the ordered pair of real numbers representing z,. It is denoted by Im or $\Im\{z\}$, where $\Im$ is a capital I in the Fraktur typeface. The complex function which maps z to the _____ of z is not holomorphic.

 a. A posteriori
 b. A Mathematical Theory of Communication
 c. A chemical equation
 d. Imaginary part

56. In mathematics, the _____ of a complex number z, is the first element of the ordered pair of real numbers representing z. It is denoted by Re{z} or $\Re\{z\}$, where $\Re$ is a capital R in the Fraktur typeface. The complex function which maps z to the _____ of z is not holomorphic.

a. 1-center problem
b. Complex number
c. 120-cell
d. Real part

Chapter 7. The Basic Concepts of Algebra

1. In abstract algebra, a field extension L /K is called _____ if every element of L is _____ over K. Field extensions which are not _____.

For example, the field extension R/Q, that is the field of real numbers as an extension of the field of rational numbers, is transcendental, while the field extensions C/R and Q

   a. Echo
   b. Identity
   c. Ideal
   d. Algebraic

2. A _____ is an algebraic equation in which each term is either a constant or the product of a constant and a single variable. _____s can have one, two, three or more variables.

   _____s occur with great regularity in applied mathematics.

   a. Quadratic equation
   b. Difference of two squares
   c. Quartic equation
   d. Linear equation

3. _____ is the mathematical operation of scaling one number by another. It is one of the four basic operations in elementary arithmetic.

   _____ is defined for whole numbers in terms of repeated addition; for example, 4 multiplied by 3 can be calculated by adding 3 copies of 4 together:

   $$4 + 4 + 4 = 12.$$

   _____ of rational numbers and real numbers is defined by systematic generalization of this basic idea.

   a. The number 0 is even.
   b. Highest common factor
   c. Multiplication
   d. Least common multiple

4. A _____ is a software program that facilitates symbolic mathematics. The core functionality of a CAS is manipulation of mathematical expressions in symbolic form.

64　　*Chapter 7. The Basic Concepts of Algebra*

The symbolic manipulations supported typically include

- simplification to the smallest possible expression or some standard form, including automatic simplification with assumptions and simplification with constraints
- substitution of symbolic, functors or numeric values for expressions
- change of form of expressions: expanding products and powers, partial and full factorization, rewriting as partial fractions, constraint satisfaction, rewriting trigonometric functions as exponentials, etc.
- partial and total differentiation
- symbolic constrained and unconstrained global optimization
- solution of linear and some non-linear equations over various domains
- solution of some differential and difference equations
- taking some limits
- some indefinite and definite integration, including multidimensional integrals
- integral transforms
- arbitrary-precision numeric operations
- Series operations such as expansion, summation and products
- matrix operations including products, inverses, etc.
- display of mathematical expressions in two-dimensional mathematical form, often using typesetting systems similar to TeX
- add-ons for use in applied mathematics such as physics packages for physical computation
- plotting graphs and parametric plots of functions in two and three dimensions, and animating them
- APIs for linking it on an external program such as a database, or using in a programming language to use the _____
- drawing charts and diagrams
- string manipulation such as matching and searching
- statistical computation
- Theorem proving and verification
- graphic production and editing such as CGI and signal processing as image processing
- sound synthesis

Many also include a programming language, allowing users to implement their own algorithms.

Some _____ s focus on a specific area of application; these are typically developed in academia and are free.

a. 120-cell　　　　　　　　　　　　　　b. Computer algebra system
c. 1-center problem　　　　　　　　　　d. 2-3 heap

5.　A _____ is a simple shape of Euclidean geometry consisting of those points in a plane which are at a constant distance, called the radius, from a fixed point, called the center. A _____ with center A is sometimes denoted by the symbol A.

A chord of a _____ is a line segment whose two endpoints lie on the _____.

a. Circle
b. Circular segment
c. Circumcircle
d. Malfatti circles

6. In the study of metric spaces in mathematics, there are various notions of two metrics on the same underlying space being 'the same', or _____.

In the following, M will denote a non-empty set and d_1 and d_2 will denote two metrics on M.

The two metrics d_1 and d_2 are said to be topologically _____ if they generate the same topology on M.

a. A chemical equation
b. A Mathematical Theory of Communication
c. Equivalent
d. A posteriori

7. Exponentiation is a mathematical operation, written a^n, involving two numbers, the base a and the _____ n. When n is a positive integer, exponentiation corresponds to repeated multiplication:

$$a^n = \underbrace{a \times \cdots \times a}_{n},$$

just as multiplication by a positive integer corresponds to repeated addition:

$$a \times n = \underbrace{a + \cdots + a}_{n}.$$

The _____ is usually shown as a superscript to the right of the base. The exponentiation a^n can be read as: a raised to the n-th power, a raised to the power [of] n or possibly a raised to the _____ [of] n, or more briefly: a to the n-th power or a to the power [of] n, or even more briefly: a to the n.

a. Exponentiating by squaring
b. Exponential tree
c. Exponential sum
d. Exponent

8. _____ is the title of a short book on logic by Gottlob Frege, published in 1879, and is also the name of the formal system set out in that book.

_____ is usually translated as concept writing or concept notation; the full title of the book identifies it as 'a formula language, modelled on that of arithmetic, of pure thought.' The _____ was arguably the most important publication in logic since Aristotle founded the subject. Frege's motivation for developing his formal approach to logic resembled Leibniz's motivation for his calculus ratiocinator.

a. 120-cell
b. 1-center problem
c. 2-3 heap
d. Begriffsschrift

9. In mathematics, and in particular in abstract algebra, distributivity is a property of binary operations that generalises the _____ law from elementary algebra.

a. General linear group
b. Distributive
c. Closure with a twist
d. Permutation

10. A _____ typically refers to a class of handheld calculators that are capable of plotting graphs, solving simultaneous equations, and performing numerous other tasks with variables. Most popular _____s are also programmable, allowing the user to create customized programs, typically for scientific/engineering and education applications. Due to their large displays intended for graphing, they can also accommodate several lines of text and calculations at a time.
   a. Genus
   b. Bump mapping
   c. Graphing calculator
   d. Support vector machines

11. A _____ is a device for performing mathematical calculations, distinguished from a computer by having a limited problem solving ability and an interface optimized for interactive calculation rather than programming. _____s can be hardware or software, and mechanical or electronic, and are often built into devices such as PDAs or mobile phones.

Modern electronic _____s are generally small, digital, and usually inexpensive.

   a. 2-3 heap
   b. Calculator
   c. 1-center problem
   d. 120-cell

12. In functional analysis, a Banach space is called _____ if it satisfies a certain abstract property involving dual spaces. _____ spaces turn out to have desirable geometric properties.

Suppose X is a normed vector space over R or C.

   a. Gamma test
   b. Copula
   c. Boolean algebra
   d. Reflexive

13. In traditional logic, an _____ or postulate is a proposition that is not proved or demonstrated but considered to be either self-evident, or subject to necessary decision. Therefore, its truth is taken for granted, and serves as a starting point for deducing and inferring other truths.

In mathematics, the term _____ is used in two related but distinguishable senses: 'logical _____s' and 'non-logical _____s'.

   a. AND-OR-Invert
   b. Algebraic logic
   c. Enumerative definition
   d. Axiom

14. _____ refers to any mathematics of the peoples of Mesopotamia, from the days of the early Sumerians to the fall of Babylon in 539 BC. In contrast to the scarcity of sources in Egyptian mathematics, our knowledge of _____ is derived from some 400 clay tablets unearthed since the 1850s. Written in Cuneiform script, tablets were inscribed while the clay was moist, and baked hard in an oven or by the heat of the sun.
   a. 1-center problem
   b. Babylonian mathematics
   c. 120-cell
   d. 2-3 heap

Chapter 7. The Basic Concepts of Algebra

15. In mathematics, a function f is _____ of a function g if f whenever A and B are complementary angles. This definition typically applies to trigonometric functions.
   a. Cofunction
   b. Balian-Low theorem
   c. Birkhoff interpolation
   d. Boxcar function

16. Suppose that φ : M → N is a smooth map between smooth manifolds; then the _____ of φ at a point x is, in some sense, the best linear approximation of φ near x. It can be viewed as generalization of the total derivative of ordinary calculus. Explicitly, it is a linear map from the tangent space of M at x to the tangent space of N at φ
   a. Concurrent
   b. Boundary
   c. Differential
   d. Grill

17. _____s arise in many problems in physics, engineering, etc. The following examples show how to solve _____s in a few simple cases when an exact solution exists.

A separable linear ordinary _____ of the first order has the general form:

$$\frac{dy}{dt} + f(t)y = 0$$

where f is some known function.

   a. Nahm equations
   b. Nullcline
   c. Differential equation
   d. Homogeneous differential equation

18. In mathematics and in the sciences, a _____ (plural: _____e, formulæ or _____s) is a concise way of expressing information symbolically (as in a mathematical or chemical _____), or a general relationship between quantities. One of many famous _____e is Albert Einstein's E = mc² (see special relativity

In mathematics, a _____ is a key to solve an equation with variables. For example, the problem of determining the volume of a sphere is one that requires a significant amount of integral calculus to solve.

   a. 1-center problem
   b. Formula
   c. 120-cell
   d. 2-3 heap

19. In ecology, predation describes a biological interaction where a _____ (an organism that is hunting) feeds on its prey, the organism that is attacked. _____s may or may not kill their prey prior to feeding on them, but the act of predation always results in the death of the prey. The other main category of consumption is detritivory, the consumption of dead organic material (detritus.)
   a. 120-cell
   b. Prey
   c. 1-center problem
   d. Predator

20. A _____ is the transfer of an interest in property (or in law the equivalent - a charge) to a lender as a security for a debt - usually a loan of money. While a _____ in itself is not a debt, it is lender's security for a debt. It is a transfer of an interest in land (or the equivalent), from the owner to the _____ lender, on the condition that this interest will be returned to the owner of the real estate when the terms of the _____ have been satisfied or performed.

a. Mortgage
b. 1-center problem
c. 2-3 heap
d. 120-cell

21. _____ was the Allied codename for any of several German teleprinter stream ciphers used during World War II. Enciphered teleprinter traffic was used between German High Command and Army Group commanders in the field, so its intelligence value was of the highest strategic value to the Allies. This traffic normally passed over landlines, but as German forces extended their reach out of western Europe, they had to resort to wireless transmission.
   a. Function
   b. Divide and conquer
   c. Colossus
   d. Fish

22. In graph theory, a _____ in a graph is a sequence of vertices such that from each of its vertices there is an edge to the next vertex in the sequence. The first vertex is called the start vertex and the last vertex is called the end vertex. Both of them are called end or terminal vertices of the _____.
   a. Blinding
   b. Deltoid
   c. Class
   d. Path

23. _____ is a general term for any type of information processing. This includes phenomena ranging from human thinking to calculations with a more narrow meaning. _____ is a process following a well-defined model that is understood and can be expressed in an algorithm, protocol, network topology, etc.
   a. 1-center problem
   b. Computation
   c. 2-3 heap
   d. 120-cell

24. _____ is a fee, paid on borrowed capital. Assets lent include money, shares, consumer goods through hire purchase, major assets such as aircraft, and even entire factories in finance lease arrangements. The _____ is calculated upon the value of the assets in the same manner as upon money.
   a. Interest expense
   b. Interest sensitivity gap
   c. A Mathematical Theory of Communication
   d. Interest

25. Leonardo of Pisa (c. 1170 - c. 1250), also known as Leonardo Pisano, Leonardo Bonacci, Leonardo _____, or, most commonly, simply _____, was an Italian mathematician, considered by some 'the most talented mathematician of the Middle Ages'.
   a. Guido Castelnuovo
   b. Harry Hinsley
   c. Ralph C. Merkle
   d. Fibonacci

26. In mathematics, an _____, or central tendency of a data set refers to a measure of the 'middle' or 'expected' value of the data set. There are many different descriptive statistics that can be chosen as a measurement of the central tendency of the data items.

An _____ is a single value that is meant to typify a list of values.

   a. A chemical equation
   b. A posteriori
   c. A Mathematical Theory of Communication
   d. Average

27. In computational complexity theory, an algorithm is said to take _____ if the asymptotic upper bound for the time it requires is proportional to the size of the input, which is usually denoted n.

Chapter 7. The Basic Concepts of Algebra 69

Informally spoken, the running time increases linearly with the size of the input. For example, a procedure that adds up all elements of a list requires time proportional to the length of the list.

a. Truth table reduction
b. Constructible function
c. Linear time
d. Time-constructible function

28. In statistics, _____ has two related meanings:

- the arithmetic _____.
- the expected value of a random variable, which is also called the population _____.

It is sometimes stated that the '_____' _____s average. This is incorrect if '_____' is taken in the specific sense of 'arithmetic _____' as there are different types of averages: the _____, median, and mode. For instance, average house prices almost always use the median value for the average.

For a real-valued random variable X, the _____ is the expectation of X.

a. Mean
b. Probability
c. Statistical population
d. Proportional hazards model

29. _____ is a special mathematical relationship between two quantities. Two quantities are called proportional if they vary in such a way that one of the quantities is a constant multiple of the other, or equivalently if they have a constant ratio.

a. Depth
b. Discontinuity
c. Proportionality
d. Compression

30. A _____ is a point in a perspective drawing to which parallel lines appear to converge. The number and placement of the _____s determines which perspective technique is being used.

- linear perspective is a drawing with 1-3 _____s.
- curvilinear perspective is a drawing with 5 _____s mapped into a circle with 4 VPs at the cardinal headings N,W,S,E and one at the circle origin.
- reverse perspective is a drawing with _____s that are placed outside the painting with the illusion that they are 'in front of' the painting.

_____s were first used by Renaissance artists such as Donatello and Masaccio.

_____s can also refer to the point in the distance where the two verges of a road appear to converge.

a. 1-center problem
b. 120-cell
c. 2-3 heap
d. Vanishing point

31. In mathematics, hyperbolic n-space, denoted H^n, is the maximally symmetric, simply connected, n-dimensional Riemannian manifold with constant sectional curvature −1. _____ is the principal example of a space exhibiting hyperbolic geometry. It can be thought of as the negative-curvature analogue of the n-sphere.

a. Margulis lemma
b. Hyperbolic geometry
c. Horocycle
d. Hyperbolic space

32. In mathematics, a _____ is a constant multiplicative factor of a certain object. For example, in the expression $9x^2$, the _____ of x^2 is 9.

The object can be such things as a variable, a vector, a function, etc.

a. Coefficient
b. Multivariate division algorithm
c. Stability radius
d. Fibonacci polynomials

33. In mathematics, the _____ of a number n is the number that, when added to n, yields zero. The _____ of n is denoted −n. For example, 7 is −7, because 7 + (−7) = 0, and the _____ of −0.3 is 0.3, because −0.3 + 0.3 = 0.

a. Additive inverse
b. Arity
c. Algebraic structure
d. Associativity

34. _____, as that term is used in this article, is the mathematics written in Greek, developed from the 6th century BC to the 5th century AD around the Eastern shores of the Mediterranean. The word 'mathematics' itself derives from the ancient Greek μαθημα, meaning 'subject of instruction'.. The study of mathematics for its own sake and the use of generalized mathematical theories and proofs is the key difference between _____ and those of preceding civilizations.

a. 1-center problem
b. 2-3 heap
c. 120-cell
d. Greek mathematics

35. In mathematics, an _____ is a statement about the relative size or order of two objects, or about whether they are the same or not

- The notation a < b means that a is less than b.
- The notation a > b means that a is greater than b.
- The notation a ≠ b means that a is not equal to b, but does not say that one is bigger than the other or even that they can be compared in size.

In all these cases, a is not equal to b, hence, '_____'.

These relations are known as strict _____

- The notation a ≤ b means that a is less than or equal to b;
- The notation a ≥ b means that a is greater than or equal to b;

An additional use of the notation is to show that one quantity is much greater than another, normally by several orders of magnitude.

- The notation a << b means that a is much less than b.
- The notation a >> b means that a is much greater than b.

Chapter 7. The Basic Concepts of Algebra

If the sense of the _____ is the same for all values of the variables for which its members are defined, then the _____ is called an 'absolute' or 'unconditional' _____. If the sense of an _____ holds only for certain values of the variables involved, but is reversed or destroyed for other values of the variables, it is called a conditional _____.

An _____ may appear unsolvable because it only states whether a number is larger or smaller than another number; but it is possible to apply the same operations for equalities to inequalities. For example, to find x for the _____ 10x > 23 one would divide 23 by 10.

    a. Inequality
    b. A Mathematical Theory of Communication
    c. A posteriori
    d. A chemical equation

36. In mathematics, a _____ is a set of real numbers with the property that any number that lies between two numbers in the set is also included in the set. For example, the set of all numbers x satisfying $0 \leq x \leq 1$ is an _____ which contains 0 and 1, as well as all numbers between them. Other examples of _____s are the set of all real numbers $\mathbb{R}$, the set of all positive real numbers, and the empty set.
    a. Interval
    b. Annihilator
    c. Ideal
    d. Order

37. _____ is the notation in which permitted values for a variable are expressed as ranging over a certain interval; "5 < x < 9" is an example of the application of _____.
    a. Interval notation
    b. Infinity
    c. A Mathematical Theory of Communication
    d. Implicit differentiation

38. In mathematics, a _____ is a picture of a straight line in which the integers are shown as specially-marked points evenly spaced on the line. Although this image only shows the integers from -9 to 9, the line includes all real numbers, continuing 'forever' in each direction. It is often used as an aid in teaching simple addition and subtraction, especially involving negative numbers.
    a. Number line
    b. Number system
    c. Real number
    d. Point plotting

39. A _____ is the large number 10^{100}, that is, the digit 1 followed by one hundred zeros. The term was coined in 1938 by Milton Sirotta, nephew of American mathematician Edward Kasner. Kasner popularized the concept in his book Mathematics and the Imagination.
    a. 120-cell
    b. Googol
    c. 2-3 heap
    d. 1-center problem

40. The _____ governs the differentiation of products of differentiable functions.
    a. Product rule
    b. 120-cell
    c. 1-center problem
    d. Reciprocal Rule

41. In mathematics, a _____ is the end result of a division problem. It can also be expressed as the number of times the divisor divides into the dividend.

a. Quotient
c. Marginal cost
b. Limiting
d. Notation

42. This article will state and prove the _____ for differentiation, and then use it to prove these two formulas.

The _____ for differentiation states that for every natural number n, the derivative of $f(x) = x^n$ is $f'(x) = nx^{n-1}$, that is,

$$(x^n)' = nx^{n-1}.$$

The _____ for integration

$$\int x^n \, dx = \frac{x^{n+1}}{n+1} + C$$

for natural n is then an easy consequence. One just needs to take the derivative of this equality and use the _____ and linearity of differentiation on the right-hand side.

a. Power rule
c. Standard part function
b. Functional integration
d. Periodic function

43. _____, also sometimes known as standard form or as exponential notation, is a way of writing numbers that accommodates values too large or small to be conveniently written in standard decimal notation. _____ has a number of useful properties and is often favored by scientists, mathematicians and engineers, who work with such numbers.

In _____, numbers are written in the form:

$$a \times 10^b$$

a. Scientific notation
c. 1-center problem
b. Leading zero
d. Radix point

44. In a positional numeral system, the decimal separator is a symbol used to mark the boundary between the integral and the fractional parts of a decimal numeral. When used in context of Arabic numerals, terms implying the symbol used are _____ and decimal comma.

The decimal separator is mathematically a radix point.

a. Hexadecimal
c. Tetradecimal
b. Fibonacci coding
d. Decimal point

Chapter 7. The Basic Concepts of Algebra

45. In mathematics, a _____ is an expression constructed from variables and constants, using the operations of addition, subtraction, multiplication, and constant non-negative whole number exponents. For example, $x^2 - 4x + 7$ is a _____, but $x^2 - 4/x + 7x^{3/2}$ is not, because its second term involves division by the variable x and also because its third term contains an exponent that is not a whole number.

_____s are one of the most important concepts in algebra and throughout mathematics and science.

   a. Group extension   b. Semifield
   c. Coimage   d. Polynomial

46. In elementary algebra, a _____ is a polynomial consisting of three terms; in other words, a _____ is the sum of three monomials. It can be factored using simple steps

In linguistics, a _____ is a fixed expression which is made from three words; e.g. 'lights, camera, action', 'signed, sealed, delivered'.

   a. Symmetric difference   b. Trinomial
   c. Recurrence relation   d. Relation algebra

47. In cryptography, the _____ was a method devised by Polish mathematician-cryptologist Jerzy Różycki, at the Polish General Staff's Cipher Bureau, to facilitate decrypting German Enigma messages. This method sometimes made it possible to determine which of the Enigma machine's rotors was at the far right, that is, in the position where the rotor always revolved at every depression of a key.

- Biuro Szyfrów

   a. Bombe   b. FROSTBURG
   c. TWIRL   d. Clock

48. In mathematics, _____ is a system of arithmetic for integers, where numbers 'wrap around' after they reach a certain value -- the modulus. _____ was introduced by Carl Friedrich Gauss in his book Disquisitiones Arithmeticae, published in 1801.

A familiar use of _____ is its use in the 24-hour clock: the arithmetic of time-keeping in which the day runs from midnight to midnight and is divided into 24 hours, numbered from 0 to 23.

   a. Modular arithmetic   b. Residue number system
   c. Multiplicative group of integers modulo n   d. Discrete logarithm

49. In elementary algebra, a _____ is a polynomial with two terms: the sum of two monomials. It is the simplest kind of polynomial except for a monomial.

The _____ a² − b² can be factored as the product of two other _____s:

a² − b² .

The product of a pair of linear _____s a x + b and c x + d is:

2 +x + bd.

A _____ raised to the nth power, represented as

n

can be expanded by means of the _____ theorem or, equivalently, using Pascal's triangle.

a. Cylindrical algebraic decomposition
c. Binomial
b. Rational root theorem
d. Real structure

50. In mathematics, a _____ is a natural number which has exactly two distinct natural number divisors: 1 and itself. An infinitude of _____s exists, as demonstrated by Euclid around 300 BC. The first twenty-five _____s are:

2, 3, 5, 7, 11, 13, 17, 19, 23, 29, 31, 37, 41, 43, 47, 53, 59, 61, 67, 71, 73, 79, 83, 89, 97.

a. Pronic number
c. Perrin number
b. Highly composite number
d. Prime number

51. In mathematics, in the realm of group theory, a group is said to be _____ if it equals its own commutator subgroup if the group has no nontrivial abelian quotients.

The smallest _____ group is the alternating group A₅. More generally, any non-abelian simple group is _____ since the commutator subgroup is a normal subgroup with abelian quotient.

a. Quaternion group
c. Group of Lie type
b. Free product
d. Perfect

52. In mathematics, a _____ is a polynomial equation of the second degree. The general form is

$$ax^2 + bx + c = 0,$$

where a ≠ 0.

The letters a, b, and c are called coefficients: the quadratic coefficient a is the coefficient of x^2, the linear coefficient b is the coefficient of x, and c is the constant coefficient, also called the free term or constant term.

Chapter 7. The Basic Concepts of Algebra

a. Linear equation
b. Quartic equation
c. Quadratic equation
d. Difference of two squares

53. In algebra, the _____ of a polynomial with real or complex coefficients is a certain expression in the coefficients of the polynomial which is equal to zero if and only if the polynomial has a multiple root in the complex numbers. For example, the _____ of the quadratic polynomial

$$ax^2 + bx + c \text{ is } b^2 - 4ac.$$

The _____ of the cubic polynomial

$$ax^3 + bx^2 + cx + d \text{ is } b^2c^2 - 4ac^3 - 4b^3d - 27a^2d^2 + 18abcd.$$

a. Jacobian conjecture
b. Boubaker polynomial
c. Square-free polynomial
d. Discriminant

54. A quadratic equation with real solutions, called roots, which may be real or complex, is given by the _____: $x = \frac{-b \pm \sqrt{b^2 - 4ac}}{2a}$.

a. Quotient
b. Parametric continuity
c. Differential Algebra
d. Quadratic formula

55. In vascular plants, the _____ is the organ of a plant body that typically lies below the surface of the soil. This is not always the case, however, since a _____ can also be aerial (that is, growing above the ground) or aerating (that is, growing up above the ground or especially above water.) Furthermore, a stem normally occurring below ground is not exceptional either

a. 2-3 heap
b. 120-cell
c. Root
d. 1-center problem

56. In mathematics, a _____ of a number x is a number r such that $r^2 = x$, or, in other words, a number r whose square is x. Every non-negative real number x has a unique non-negative _____, called the principal _____, which is denoted with a radical symbol as $\sqrt{x}$, or, using exponent notation, as $x^{1/2}$. For example, the principal _____ of 9 is 3, denoted $\sqrt{9} = 3$, because $3^2 = 3 \times 3 = 9$.

a. Double exponential
b. Hyperbolic functions
c. Multiplicative inverse
d. Square root

57. In mathematics and the arts, two quantities are in the _____ if the ratio between the sum of those quantities and the larger one is the same as the ratio between the larger one and the smaller. The _____ is an irrational mathematical constant, approximately 1.6180339887.

At least since the Renaissance, many artists and architects have proportioned their works to approximate the _____ -- especially in the form of the golden rectangle, in which the ratio of the longer side to the shorter is the _____ --believing this proportion to be aesthetically pleasing.

a. 1-center problem
c. 2-3 heap
b. 120-cell
d. Golden ratio

Chapter 8. Graphs, Functions, and Systems of Equations and Inequalities

1. In quantum field theory and statistical mechanics in the thermodynamic limit, a system with a global symmetry can have more than one phase. For parameters where the symmetry is spontaneously broken, the system is said to be _____. When the global symmetry is unbroken the system is disordered.

    a. Ursell function
    b. Einstein relation
    c. Isoenthalpic-isobaric ensemble
    d. Ordered

2. In mathematics, an _____ is a collection of objects having two coordinates (or entries or projections), such that one can always uniquely determine the object, which is the first coordinate (or first entry or left projection) of the pair as well as the second coordinate (or second entry or right projection.) If the first coordinate is a and the second is b, the usual notation for an _____ is (a, b.) The pair is 'ordered' in that (a, b) differs from (b, a) unless a = b.

    a. A posteriori
    b. A chemical equation
    c. A Mathematical Theory of Communication
    d. Ordered pair

3. In mathematics, the _____ of a Euclidean space is a special point, usually denoted by the letter O, used as a fixed point of reference for the geometry of the surrounding space. In a Cartesian coordinate system, the _____ is the point where the axes of the system intersect. In Euclidean geometry, the _____ may be chosen freely as any convenient point of reference.

    a. Autonomous system
    b. Interval
    c. Origin
    d. OMAC

4. In mathematics, the _____ or Pythagoras' theorem is a relation in Euclidean geometry among the three sides of a right triangle. The theorem is named after the Greek mathematician Pythagoras, who by tradition is credited with its discovery and proof, although it is often argued that knowledge of the theory predates him.. The theorem is as follows:

    In any right triangle, the area of the square whose side is the hypotenuse is equal to the sum of the areas of the squares whose sides are the two legs.

    a. Pythagorean theorem
    b. 2-3 heap
    c. 1-center problem
    d. 120-cell

5. A _____ consists of one quarter of the coordinate plane.

    a. 2-3 heap
    b. 1-center problem
    c. Quadrant
    d. 120-cell

6. A _____ is a software program that facilitates symbolic mathematics. The core functionality of a CAS is manipulation of mathematical expressions in symbolic form.

The symbolic manipulations supported typically include

- simplification to the smallest possible expression or some standard form, including automatic simplification with assumptions and simplification with constraints
- substitution of symbolic, functors or numeric values for expressions
- change of form of expressions: expanding products and powers, partial and full factorization, rewriting as partial fractions, constraint satisfaction, rewriting trigonometric functions as exponentials, etc.
- partial and total differentiation
- symbolic constrained and unconstrained global optimization
- solution of linear and some non-linear equations over various domains
- solution of some differential and difference equations
- taking some limits
- some indefinite and definite integration, including multidimensional integrals
- integral transforms
- arbitrary-precision numeric operations
- Series operations such as expansion, summation and products
- matrix operations including products, inverses, etc.
- display of mathematical expressions in two-dimensional mathematical form, often using typesetting systems similar to TeX
- add-ons for use in applied mathematics such as physics packages for physical computation
- plotting graphs and parametric plots of functions in two and three dimensions, and animating them
- APIs for linking it on an external program such as a database, or using in a programming language to use the _____
- drawing charts and diagrams
- string manipulation such as matching and searching
- statistical computation
- Theorem proving and verification
- graphic production and editing such as CGI and signal processing as image processing
- sound synthesis

Many also include a programming language, allowing users to implement their own algorithms.

Some _____s focus on a specific area of application; these are typically developed in academia and are free.

a. 2-3 heap
c. 1-center problem
b. 120-cell
d. Computer algebra system

7. In mathematics and in the sciences, a _____ (plural: _____e, formulæ or _____s) is a concise way of expressing information symbolically (as in a mathematical or chemical _____), or a general relationship between quantities. One of many famous _____e is Albert Einstein's $E = mc^2$ (see special relativity)

In mathematics, a _____ is a key to solve an equation with variables. For example, the problem of determining the volume of a sphere is one that requires a significant amount of integral calculus to solve.

Chapter 8. Graphs, Functions, and Systems of Equations and Inequalities   79

    a. 1-center problem   b. 2-3 heap
    c. 120-cell   d. Formula

8. In mathematics, a _____ is a statement that can be proved on the basis of explicitly stated or previously agreed assumptions.
    a. Boolean function   b. Disjunction introduction
    c. Logical value   d. Theorem

9. The _____ is the horizontal axis of a two- dimensional plot in the Cartesian coordinate system, that is typically pointed to the right. Also known as a right-handed coordinate system.
    a. 1-center problem   b. 120-cell
    c. 2-3 heap   d. X-axis

10. In reference to a 2D and 3D plane, the _____ is the vertical height of a 2D or 3D object.
    a. 2-3 heap   b. 120-cell
    c. 1-center problem   d. Y-axis

11. _____ is a branch of mathematics that includes the study of limits, derivatives, integrals, and infinite series, and constitutes a major part of modern university education. Historically, it has been referred to as 'the _____ of infinitesimals', or 'infinitesimal _____'. Most basically, _____ is the study of change, in the same way that geometry is the study of space.
    a. Partial sum   b. Hyperbolic angle
    c. Test for Divergence   d. Calculus

12. The term _____ or centre is used in various contexts in abstract algebra to denote the set of all those elements that commute with all other elements. More specifically:

- The _____ of a group G consists of all those elements x in G such that xg = gx for all g in G. This is a normal subgroup of G.
- The _____ of a ring R is the subset of R consisting of all those elements x of R such that xr = rx for all r in R. The _____ is a commutative subring of R, so R is an algebra over its _____.
- The _____ of an algebra A consists of all those elements x of A such that xa = ax for all a in A. See also: central simple algebra.
- The _____ of a Lie algebra L consists of all those elements x in L such that [x,a] = 0 for all a in L. This is an ideal of the Lie algebra L.
- The _____ of a monoidal category C consists of pairs *a natural isomorphism satisfying certain axioms.*

    a. Disk   b. Block size
    c. Brute Force   d. Center

13. In classical geometry, a _____ of a circle or sphere is any line segment from its center to its boundary. By extension, the _____ of a circle or sphere is the length of any such segment. The _____ is half the diameter. In science and engineering the term _____ of curvature is commonly used as a synonym for _____.

a. Radius
b. Birational geometry
c. Non-Euclidean geometry
d. Duoprism

14. A _____ is a simple shape of Euclidean geometry consisting of those points in a plane which are at a constant distance, called the radius, from a fixed point, called the center. A _____ with center A is sometimes denoted by the symbol A.

A chord of a _____ is a line segment whose two endpoints lie on the _____.

a. Malfatti circles
b. Circumcircle
c. Circular segment
d. Circle

15. A _____ is an algebraic equation in which each term is either a constant or the product of a constant and a single variable. _____s can have one, two, three or more variables.

_____s occur with great regularity in applied mathematics.

a. Linear equation
b. Quartic equation
c. Difference of two squares
d. Quadratic equation

16. In mathematics, the _____ is an approach to finding a particular solution to certain inhomogeneous ordinary differential equations and recurrence relations. It is closely related to the annihilator method, but instead of using a particular kind of differential operator in order to find the best possible form of the particular solution, a 'guess' is made as to the appropriate form, which is then tested by differentiating the resulting equation. In this sense, the _____ is less formal but more intuitive than the annihilator method.

a. Differential algebraic equations
b. Phase line
c. Linear differential equation
d. Method of undetermined coefficients

17. _____ is used to describe the steepness, incline, gradient, or grade of a straight line. A higher _____ value indicates a steeper incline. The _____ is defined as the ratio of the 'rise' divided by the 'run' between two points on a line, or in other words, the ratio of the altitude change to the horizontal distance between any two points on the line.

a. Point plotting
b. Number line
c. Slope
d. Cognitively Guided Instruction

18. A _____ of a curve is the envelope of a family of congruent circles centered on the curve. It generalises the concept of _____ lines.

It is sometimes called the offset curve but the term 'offset' often refers also to translation.

a. Parallel
b. Cycloid
c. Bifolium
d. Cissoid

19. The existence and properties of _____ are the basis of Euclid's parallel postulate. _____ are two lines on the same plane that do not intersect even assuming that lines extend to infinity in either direction.

Chapter 8. Graphs, Functions, and Systems of Equations and Inequalities

  a. Square wheel
  b. Vertical translation
  c. Spidron
  d. Parallel lines

20. In mathematics, an _____, or central tendency of a data set refers to a measure of the 'middle' or 'expected' value of the data set. There are many different descriptive statistics that can be chosen as a measurement of the central tendency of the data items.

An _____ is a single value that is meant to typify a list of values.

  a. A posteriori
  b. A Mathematical Theory of Communication
  c. Average
  d. A chemical equation

21. The _____ expresses the fact that the difference in the y coordinate between two points on a line that is, y − y1 is proportional to the difference in the x coordinate that is, x − x1. The proportionality constant is m (the slope of the line).
  a. Square function
  b. Rubin Causal Model
  c. Cobb-Douglas
  d. Point-slope form

22. _____ is a form where m is the slope of the line and b is the y-intercept, which is the y-coordinate of the point where the line crosses the y axis. This can be seen by letting x = 0, which immediately gives y = b.
  a. Separable extension
  b. Dynamical system
  c. Commutative law
  d. Slope-intercept form

23. In statistics, given a sample $(Y_i, X_{i1}, \ldots, X_{ip}), i = 1, \ldots, n$ the most general form of _____ is formulated as

$$Y_i = \beta_0 + \beta_1 \phi_1(X_{i1}) + \ldots + \beta_p \phi_p(X_{ip}) + \varepsilon_i \quad i = 1, \ldots, n$$

where $\phi_1, \ldots, \phi_p$ may be nonlinear functions.

In matrix notation this model can be written as

$$Y = X\beta + \varepsilon$$

where Y is an n × 1 column vector, X is an n × matrix, β is a × 1 vector of parameters, and ε is an n × 1 vector of errors, which are uncorrelated random variables each with expected value 0 and variance σ^2. Note that depending on the context the sample can be seen as fixed, or random.

  a. Risk aversion
  b. Risk measure
  c. Life table
  d. Linear model

24. In graph theory, a _____ in a graph is a sequence of vertices such that from each of its vertices there is an edge to the next vertex in the sequence. The first vertex is called the start vertex and the last vertex is called the end vertex. Both of them are called end or terminal vertices of the _____.

Chapter 8. Graphs, Functions, and Systems of Equations and Inequalities

    a. Class
    b. Blinding
    c. Deltoid
    d. Path

25. The mathematical concept of a _____ expresses the intuitive idea of deterministic dependence between two quantities, one of which is viewed as primary and the other as secondary. A _____ then is a way to associate a unique output for each input of a specified type, for example, a real number or an element of a given set.
    a. Function
    b. Coherent
    c. Going up
    d. Grill

26. Dependent variables and _____ refer to values that change in relationship to each other. The dependent variables are those that are observed to change in response to the _____. The _____ are those that are deliberately manipulated to invoke a change in the dependent variables.
    a. Independent variables
    b. Experimental design diagram
    c. One-factor-at-a-time method
    d. Operational confound

27. A _____ is the transfer of an interest in property (or in law the equivalent - a charge) to a lender as a security for a debt - usually a loan of money. While a _____ in itself is not a debt, it is lender's security for a debt. It is a transfer of an interest in land (or the equivalent), from the owner to the _____ lender, on the condition that this interest will be returned to the owner of the real estate when the terms of the _____ have been satisfied or performed.
    a. 2-3 heap
    b. 120-cell
    c. 1-center problem
    d. Mortgage

28. In mathematics, especially in the area of abstract algebra known as ring theory, a _____ is a ring with $0 \neq 1$ such that $ab = 0$ implies that either $a = 0$ or $b = 0$. That is, it is a nontrivial ring without left or right zero divisors. A commutative _____ is called an integral _____.
    a. Left primitive ring
    b. Domain
    c. Modular representation theory
    d. Simple ring

29. In descriptive statistics, the _____ is the length of the smallest interval which contains all the data. It is calculated by subtracting the smallest observations from the greatest and provides an indication of statistical dispersion.

It is measured in the same units as the data.

    a. Range
    b. Bandwidth
    c. Class
    d. Kernel

30. In ecology, predation describes a biological interaction where a _____ (an organism that is hunting) feeds on its prey, the organism that is attacked. _____s may or may not kill their prey prior to feeding on them, but the act of predation always results in the death of the prey. The other main category of consumption is detritivory, the consumption of dead organic material (detritus.)
    a. Prey
    b. 1-center problem
    c. Predator
    d. 120-cell

31. In mathematics, the _____ is a conic section, the intersection of a right circular conical surface and a plane parallel to a generating straight line of that surface. Given a point and a line that lie in a plane, the locus of points in that plane that are equidistant to them is a _____.

Chapter 8. Graphs, Functions, and Systems of Equations and Inequalities

A particular case arises when the plane is tangent to the conical surface of a circle.

   a. Dandelin sphere   b. Directrix
   c. Matrix representation of conic sections   d. Parabola

32. A _____, in mathematics, is a polynomial function of the form $f(x) = ax^2 + bx + c$, where $a \neq 0$. The graph of a _____ is a parabola whose major axis is parallel to the y-axis.

The expression $ax^2 + bx + c$ in the definition of a _____ is a polynomial of degree 2 or a 2nd degree polynomial, because the highest exponent of x is 2.

   a. Multivariate division algorithm   b. Discriminant
   c. Laguerre polynomials   d. Quadratic function

33. In geometry, a _____ is a special kind of point, usually a corner of a polygon, polyhedron, or higher dimensional polytope. In the geometry of curves a _____ is a point of where the first derivative of curvature is zero. In graph theory, a _____ is the fundamental unit out of which graphs are formed
   a. Dini   b. Crib
   c. Vertex   d. Duality

34. In geometry and trigonometry, an _____ is the figure formed by two rays sharing a common endpoint, called the vertex of the _____. The magnitude of the _____ is the 'amount of rotation' that separates the two rays, and can be measured by considering the length of circular arc swept out when one ray is rotated about the vertex to coincide with the other. Where there is no possibility of confusion, the term '_____' is used interchangeably for both the geometric configuration itself and for its angular magnitude.
   a. A posteriori   b. Angle
   c. A Mathematical Theory of Communication   d. A chemical equation

35. _____ is the interpreting of the meaning of a text and the subsequent production of an equivalent text, likewise called a '_____,' that communicates the same message in another language. The text to be translated is called the 'source text,' and the language that it is to be translated into is called the 'target language'; the final product is sometimes called the 'target text.'

_____ must take into account constraints that include context, the rules of grammar of the two languages, their writing conventions, and their idioms. A common misconception is that there exists a simple word-for-word correspondence between any two languages, and that _____ is a straightforward mechanical process; such a word-for-word _____, however, cannot take into account context, grammar, conventions, and idioms.

   a. 2-3 heap   b. 120-cell
   c. 1-center problem   d. Translation

36. In mathematics an _____ , a 'falling short') is a conic section, the locus of points in a plane such that the sum of the distances to two fixed points is equal to a given constant. The two fixed points are then called foci.

Chapter 8. Graphs, Functions, and Systems of Equations and Inequalities

Another way is to define it as the path traced out by a point whose distance from a focus maintains a constant ratio less than one with its distance from a straight line not passing through the focus, called the directrix.

a. A chemical equation
b. A Mathematical Theory of Communication
c. Ellipse
d. A posteriori

37. In cryptography, _____ is a pseudorandom number generator and a stream cipher designed by Robert Jenkins to be cryptographically secure. The name is an acronym for Indirection, Shift, Accumulate, Add, and Count.

The _____ algorithm has similarities with RC4.

a. Order
b. Introduction
c. Imputation
d. Isaac

38. The _____ (symbol: N) is the SI derived unit of force, named after Isaac _____ in recognition of his work on classical mechanics.

The _____ is the unit of force derived in the SI system; it is equal to the amount of force required to accelerate a mass of one kilogram at a rate of one meter per second per second. Algebraically:

$$1\ N = 1\ \frac{kg \cdot m}{s^2}.$$

- 1 N is the force of Earth's gravity on an object with a mass of about 102 g ($1/_{9.8}$ kg) (such as a small apple.)
- On Earth's surface, a mass of 1 kg exerts a force of approximately 9.80665 N [down] (or 1 kgf.) The approximation of 1 kg corresponding to 10 N is sometimes used as a rule of thumb in everyday life and in engineering.
- The force of Earth's gravity on a human being with a mass of 70 kg is approximately 687 N.
- The dot product of force and distance is mechanical work. Thus, in SI units, a force of 1 N exerted over a distance of 1 m is 1 NÂ·m of work. The Work-Energy Theorem states that the work done on a body is equal to the change in energy of the body. 1 NÂ·m = 1 J (joule), the SI unit of energy.
- It is common to see forces expressed in kilonewtons or kN, where 1 kN = 1 000 N.

a. 2-3 heap
b. 120-cell
c. Newton
d. 1-center problem

39. _____ methods are common techniques to compute the equilibrium configuration of molecules. The basic idea is that a stable state of a molecular system should correspond to a local minimum of their potential energy. This kind of calculation generally starts from an arbitrary state of molecules, then the mathematical procedure of optimization allows us to move atoms in a way to reduce the net forces to nearly zero.

Chapter 8. Graphs, Functions, and Systems of Equations and Inequalities

a. A chemical equation
b. A Mathematical Theory of Communication
c. A posteriori
d. Energy minimization

40. In category theory, an abstract branch of mathematics, an _____ of a category C is an object I in C such that for every object X in C, there exists precisely one morphism I → X. The dual notion is that of a terminal object: T is terminal if for every object X in C there exists a single morphism X → T. _____s are also called coterminal, and terminal objects are also called final.

a. A posteriori
b. A Mathematical Theory of Communication
c. A chemical equation
d. Initial object

41. The _____ is a function in mathematics. The application of this function to a value x is written as ex. Equivalently, this can be written in the form e^x, where e is a mathematical constant, the base of the natural logarithm, which equals approximately 2.718281828, and is also known as Euler's number.

a. A chemical equation
b. A Mathematical Theory of Communication
c. Area hyperbolic functions
d. Exponential function

42. An _____ of a real-valued function y = f(x) is a curve which describes the behavior of f as either x or y tends to infinity.

In other words, as one moves along the graph of f(x) in some direction, the distance between it and the _____ eventually becomes smaller than any distance that one may specify.

If a curve A has the curve B as an _____, one says that A is asymptotic to B. Similarly B is asymptotic to A, so A and B are called asymptotic.

a. Infinite product
b. Asymptote
c. Isoperimetric dimension
d. Improper integral

43. Suppose f is a function. Then the line y = a is a _____ for f if

$$\lim_{x \to \infty} f(x) = a \text{ or } \lim_{x \to -\infty} f(x) = a.$$

Intuitively, this means that f(x) can be made as close as desired to a by making x big enough. How big is big enough depends on how close one wishes to make f(x) to a.

a. 1-center problem
b. 120-cell
c. 2-3 heap
d. Horizontal asymptote

44. A _____ typically refers to a class of handheld calculators that are capable of plotting graphs, solving simultaneous equations, and performing numerous other tasks with variables. Most popular _____s are also programmable, allowing the user to create customized programs, typically for scientific/engineering and education applications. Due to their large displays intended for graphing, they can also accommodate several lines of text and calculations at a time.

Chapter 8. Graphs, Functions, and Systems of Equations and Inequalities

   a. Graphing calculator
   b. Support vector machines
   c. Bump mapping
   d. Genus

45. _____ is a fee, paid on borrowed capital. Assets lent include money, shares, consumer goods through hire purchase, major assets such as aircraft, and even entire factories in finance lease arrangements. The _____ is calculated upon the value of the assets in the same manner as upon money.
   a. Interest expense
   b. Interest sensitivity gap
   c. A Mathematical Theory of Communication
   d. Interest

46. A _____ is a device for performing mathematical calculations, distinguished from a computer by having a limited problem solving ability and an interface optimized for interactive calculation rather than programming. _____s can be hardware or software, and mechanical or electronic, and are often built into devices such as PDAs or mobile phones.

Modern electronic _____s are generally small, digital, and usually inexpensive.

   a. Calculator
   b. 2-3 heap
   c. 120-cell
   d. 1-center problem

47. _____ is the concept of adding accumulated interest back to the principal, so that interest is earned on interest from that moment on. The act of declaring interest to be principal is called compounding. A loan, for example, may have its interest compounded every month: in this case, a loan with $100 principal and 1% interest per month would have a balance of $101 at the end of the first month.
   a. Net interest margin securities
   b. Net interest margin
   c. Retained interest
   d. Compound Interest

48. In mathematics, the _____ functions are functions of an angle; they are important when studying triangles and modeling periodic phenomena, among many other applications.
   a. Gudermannian function
   b. Coversine
   c. Trigonometric
   d. Law of sines

49. In mathematics, the _____ are functions of an angle. They are important in the study of triangles and modeling periodic phenomena, among many other applications. _____ are commonly defined as ratios of two sides of a right triangle containing the angle, and can equivalently be defined as the lengths of various line segments from a unit circle.
   a. Sine
   b. Trigonometric functions
   c. Law of sines
   d. Trigonometric integrals

50. _____ occurs when the growth rate of a mathematical function is proportional to the function's current value. In the case of a discrete domain of definition with equal intervals it is also called geometric growth or geometric decay.

With _____ of a positive value its rate of increase steadily increases, or in the case of exponential decay, its rate of decrease steadily decreases.

   a. Exponential growth
   b. A Mathematical Theory of Communication
   c. A posteriori
   d. A chemical equation

Chapter 8. Graphs, Functions, and Systems of Equations and Inequalities

51. The function $\log_b(x)$ depends on both b and x, but the term _____ (or logarithmic function) in standard usage refers to a function of the form $\log_b(x)$ in which the base b is fixed and so the only argument is x. Thus there is one _____ for each value of the base b (which must be positive and must differ from 1.) Viewed in this way, the base-b _____ is the inverse function of the exponential function b^x.

   a. 120-cell
   b. 2-3 heap
   c. 1-center problem
   d. Logarithm function

52. _____ IPA: [pjɛːʁ ɛ dᵊfɛːʁ 'ma] (17 August 1601 or 1607/8 - 12 January 1665) was a French lawyer at the Parlement of Toulouse, France, and a mathematician who is given credit for early developments that led to modern calculus. In particular, he is recognized for his discovery of an original method of finding the greatest and the smallest ordinates of curved lines, which is analogous to that of the then unknown differential calculus, as well as his research into the theory of numbers. He also made notable contributions to analytic geometry, probability, and optics.

   a. Felix Hausdorff
   b. Nikita Borisov
   c. Philip J. Davis
   d. Pierre de Fermat

53. A quantity is said to be subject to _____ if it decreases at a rate proportional to its value. Symbolically, this can be expressed as the following differential equation, where N is the quantity and λ is a positive number called the decay constant.

$$\frac{dN}{dt} = -\lambda N.$$

The solution to this equation is:

$$N(t) = N_0 e^{-\lambda t}.$$

Here is the quantity at time t, and $N_0 = N$ is the quantity, at time t = 0.

   a. Exponential formula
   b. Exponential integral
   c. Exponential decay
   d. Exponentiating by squaring

54. The _____ of a quantity whose value decreases with time is the interval required for the quantity to decay to half of its initial value. The concept originated in describing how long it takes atoms to undergo radioactive decay, but also applies in a wide variety of other situations.

The term '_____' dates to 1907.

   a. 120-cell
   b. Radioactive decay
   c. 1-center problem
   d. Half-life

55. In mathematics, the _____ of a number to a given base is the power or exponent to which the base must be raised in order to produce the number.

For example, the _____ of 1000 to the base 10 is 3, because 3 is how many 10s one must multiply to get 1000: thus 10 × 10 × 10 = 1000; the base-2 _____ of 32 is 5 because 5 is how many 2s one must multiply to get 32: thus 2 × 2 × 2 × 2 × 2 = 32. In the language of exponents: 10^3 = 1000, so $\log_{10} 1000$ = 3, and 2^5 = 32, so $\log_2 32$ = 5.

a. 1-center problem
b. 120-cell
c. 2-3 heap
d. Logarithm

56. A _____ is a mathematical model of a system based on the use of a linear operator. _____s typically exhibit features and properties that are much simpler than the general, nonlinear case. As a mathematical abstraction or idealization, _____s find important applications in automatic control theory, signal processing, and telecommunications.

a. Hybrid system
b. Percolation
c. Predispositioning Theory
d. Linear system

57. In linear algebra, the _____ of a matrix is obtained by changing a matrix in some way.

Given the matrices A and B, where:

$$A = \begin{bmatrix} 1 & 3 & 2 \\ 2 & 0 & 1 \\ 5 & 2 & 2 \end{bmatrix}, \quad B = \begin{bmatrix} 4 \\ 3 \\ 1 \end{bmatrix}$$

Then, the _____ is written as:

$$(A|B) = \begin{bmatrix} 1 & 3 & 2 & 4 \\ 2 & 0 & 1 & 3 \\ 5 & 2 & 2 & 1 \end{bmatrix}$$

This is useful when solving systems of linear equations or the _____ may also be used to find the inverse of a matrix by combining it with the identity matrix.

$$C = \begin{bmatrix} 1 & 3 \\ -5 & 0 \end{bmatrix}$$

Let C be a square 2×2 matrix where

To find the inverse of C we create where I is the 2×2 identity matrix.

a. Eigendecomposition
b. Unimodular polynomial matrix
c. Alternating sign matrix
d. Augmented matrix

58. In mathematics, a _____ is a rectangular table of elements, which may be numbers or, more generally, any abstract quantities that can be added and multiplied. Matrices are used to describe linear equations, keep track of the coefficients of linear transformations and to record data that depend on multiple parameters. Matrices are described by the field of _____ theory.

Chapter 8. Graphs, Functions, and Systems of Equations and Inequalities

a. Matrix
b. Double counting
c. Compression
d. Coherent

59. In linear algebra, _____ is a version of Gaussian elimination that puts zeros both above and below each pivot element as it goes from the top row of the given matrix to the bottom. In other words, _____ brings a matrix to reduced row echelon form, whereas Gaussian elimination takes it only as far as row echelon form. Every matrix has a reduced row echelon form, and this algorithm is guaranteed to produce it.

a. Conservation form
b. Gauss-Jordan elimination
c. Spheroidal wave functions
d. Lax equivalence theorem

60. In mathematics, specifically in combinatorial commutative algebra, a convex lattice polytope P is called _____ if it has the following property: given any positive integer n, every lattice point of the dilation nP, obtained from P by scaling its vertices by the factor n and taking the convex hull of the resulting points, can be written as the sum of exactly n lattice points in P. This property plays an important role in the theory of toric varieties, where it corresponds to projective normality of the toric variety determined by P.

The simplex in R^k with the vertices at the origin and along the unit coordinate vectors is _____.

a. Demihypercubes
b. Polytetrahedron
c. Hypercube
d. Normal

61. In mathematics, the concept of a _____ tries to capture the intuitive idea of a geometrical one-dimensional and continuous object. A simple example is the circle. In everyday use of the term '_____', a straight line is not curved, but in mathematical parlance _____s include straight lines and line segments.

a. Kappa curve
b. Quadrifolium
c. Negative pedal curve
d. Curve

62. In mathematics, an _____ is a statement about the relative size or order of two objects, or about whether they are the same or not

- The notation a < b means that a is less than b.
- The notation a > b means that a is greater than b.
- The notation a ≠ b means that a is not equal to b, but does not say that one is bigger than the other or even that they can be compared in size.

In all these cases, a is not equal to b, hence, '_____'.

These relations are known as strict _____

- The notation a ≤ b means that a is less than or equal to b;
- The notation a ≥ b means that a is greater than or equal to b;

Chapter 8. Graphs, Functions, and Systems of Equations and Inequalities

An additional use of the notation is to show that one quantity is much greater than another, normally by several orders of magnitude.

- The notation a << b means that a is much less than b.
- The notation a >> b means that a is much greater than b.

If the sense of the _____ is the same for all values of the variables for which its members are defined, then the _____ is called an 'absolute' or 'unconditional' _____. If the sense of an _____ holds only for certain values of the variables involved, but is reversed or destroyed for other values of the variables, it is called a conditional _____.

An _____ may appear unsolvable because it only states whether a number is larger or smaller than another number; but it is possible to apply the same operations for equalities to inequalities. For example, to find x for the _____ 10x > 23 one would divide 23 by 10.

a. Inequality
b. A Mathematical Theory of Communication
c. A chemical equation
d. A posteriori

63. In mathematics, _____ is a technique for optimization of a linear objective function, subject to linear equality and linear inequality constraints. Informally, _____ determines the way to achieve the best outcome in a given mathematical model given some list of requirements represented as linear equations.

More formally, given a polytope, and a real-valued affine function

$$f(x_1, x_2, \ldots, x_n) = c_1 x_1 + c_2 x_2 + \cdots + c_n x_n + d$$

defined on this polytope, a _____ method will find a point in the polytope where this function has the smallest value.

a. Linear programming relaxation
b. Descent direction
c. Lin-Kernighan
d. Linear programming

64. An _____ is a tree data structure in which each internal node has up to eight children. _____s are most often used to partition a three dimensional space by recursively subdividing it into eight octants. _____s are the three-dimensional analog of quadtrees.

a. Interval tree
b. Adaptive k-d tree
c. External node
d. Octree

65. _____ in North America, South Africa and Australia, and Operational Research in Europe, is an interdisciplinary branch of applied mathematics and formal science that uses methods such as mathematical modeling, statistics, and algorithms to arrive at optimal or near optimal solutions to complex problems. It is typically concerned with optimizing the maxima or minima of some objective function. _____ helps management achieve its goals using scientific methods.

a. A Mathematical Theory of Communication
c. A posteriori

b. A chemical equation
d. Operations research

Chapter 9. Geometry

1. _____, as that term is used in this article, is the mathematics written in Greek, developed from the 6th century BC to the 5th century AD around the Eastern shores of the Mediterranean. The word 'mathematics' itself derives from the ancient Greek μαθημα, meaning 'subject of instruction'.. The study of mathematics for its own sake and the use of generalized mathematical theories and proofs is the key difference between _____ and those of preceding civilizations.
    a. 2-3 heap
    b. 120-cell
    c. 1-center problem
    d. Greek mathematics

2. In mathematics, the _____ is an approach to finding a particular solution to certain inhomogeneous ordinary differential equations and recurrence relations. It is closely related to the annihilator method, but instead of using a particular kind of differential operator in order to find the best possible form of the particular solution, a 'guess' is made as to the appropriate form, which is then tested by differentiating the resulting equation. In this sense, the _____ is less formal but more intuitive than the annihilator method.
    a. Phase line
    b. Differential algebraic equations
    c. Linear differential equation
    d. Method of undetermined coefficients

3. In mathematics, a _____ is, informally, an infinitely vast and infinitely thin sheet. _____s may be thought of as objects in some higher dimensional space, or they may be considered without any outside space, as in the setting of Euclidean geometry
    a. Blocking
    b. Bandwidth
    c. Group
    d. Plane

4. In mathematics, _____ are two-dimensional manifolds or surfaces that are perfectly flat.
    a. Planes
    b. 2-3 heap
    c. 1-center problem
    d. 120-cell

5. A _____ of a curve is the envelope of a family of congruent circles centered on the curve. It generalises the concept of _____ lines.

It is sometimes called the offset curve but the term 'offset' often refers also to translation.

   a. Cycloid
   b. Cissoid
   c. Bifolium
   d. Parallel

6. The existence and properties of _____ are the basis of Euclid's parallel postulate. _____ are two lines on the same plane that do not intersect even assuming that lines extend to infinity in either direction.
   a. Spidron
   b. Parallel lines
   c. Square wheel
   d. Vertical translation

7. In geometry and trigonometry, an _____ is the figure formed by two rays sharing a common endpoint, called the vertex of the _____. The magnitude of the _____ is the 'amount of rotation' that separates the two rays, and can be measured by considering the length of circular arc swept out when one ray is rotated about the vertex to coincide with the other. Where there is no possibility of confusion, the term '_____' is used interchangeably for both the geometric configuration itself and for its angular magnitude.
   a. A posteriori
   b. A chemical equation
   c. A Mathematical Theory of Communication
   d. Angle

8. _____ is a part of mathematics concerned with questions of size, shape, and relative position of figures and with properties of space. _____ is one of the oldest sciences. Initially a body of practical knowledge concerning lengths, areas, and volumes, in the third century BC _____ was put into an axiomatic form by Euclid, whose treatment--Euclidean _____--set a standard for many centuries to follow.
  a. 1-center problem
  b. 2-3 heap
  c. 120-cell
  d. Geometry

9. In geometry, a _____ is a special kind of point, usually a corner of a polygon, polyhedron, or higher dimensional polytope. In the geometry of curves a _____ is a point of where the first derivative of curvature is zero. In graph theory, a _____ is the fundamental unit out of which graphs are formed
  a. Duality
  b. Crib
  c. Dini
  d. Vertex

10. A _____ is a movement of an object in a circular motion. A two-dimensional object rotates around a center of _____. A three-dimensional object rotates around a line called an axis.
  a. Steiner-Lehmus theorem
  b. Square lattice
  c. Homothetic center
  d. Rotation

11. _____ or _____ lines lie on different planes. They are neither parallel nor intersecting.

- In geometry, straight lines in a space referred to as _____ if they are neither parallel nor intersecting.
- In statistics, _____ is sometimes used as an alternative term to skewness to refer to the degree of asymmetry of a distribution. It can mean distortion in a positive or negative direction.
- In parallel transmission, the difference in arrival time of bits transmitted at the same time.
- For data recorded on multichannel magnetic tape, the difference between reading times of bits recorded in a single transverse line.

Nte: _____ is usually interpreted to mean the difference in reading times between bits recorded on the tracks at the extremities, or edges, of the tape.

  a. P-wave
  b. Common operator notation
  c. Skew
  d. Genus

12. An angle smaller than a right angle is called an _____ (less than 90 degrees).
  a. Euclidean geometry
  b. Integral geometry
  c. Ultraparallel theorem
  d. Acute angle

13. In geometry and trigonometry, a _____ is defined as an angle between two straight intersecting lines of ninety degrees, or one-quarter of a circle.
  a. Trigonometry
  b. Trigonometric functions
  c. Sine integral
  d. Right angle

14. An angle equal to two right angles is called a _____ (equal to 180 degrees).

a. Loomis-Whitney inequality
b. Straight angle
c. Householder transformation
d. Theorem

15. A pair of angles are said to be _____ if they share the same vertex and are bounded by the same pair of lines but are opposite to each other. They are also congruent.
   a. Vertical angles
   b. Reflection symmetry
   c. Line segment
   d. Hinge theorem

16. A pair of angles is _____ if their measurements add up to 180 degrees. If the two _____ angles are adjacent their non-shared sides form a straight line. The supplement of 135 would be 45.
   a. Dense
   b. FISH
   c. Cylinder
   d. Supplementary

17. A pair of angles are complementary if the sum of their measures add up to 90 degrees.

If the two _____ are adjacent (i.e. have a common vertex and share a side, but do not have any interior points in common) their non-shared sides form a right angle.

In Euclidean geometry, the two acute angles in a right triangle are complementary, because there are 180>° in a triangle and 90>° have been accounted for by the right angle.

   a. Complementary Angles
   b. Quincunx
   c. Conway polyhedron notation
   d. Hypotenuse

18. In combinatorial mathematics, given a collection C of sets, a _____ is a set containing exactly one element from each member of the collection: it is a section of the quotient map induced by the collection. If the original sets are not disjoint, there are several different definitions. One variation is that there is a bijection f from the _____ to C such that x is an element of f
   a. Combinatorial design
   b. Combinadic
   c. Heawood number
   d. Transversal

19. A _____, from the French patron, is a type of theme of recurring events of or objects, sometimes referred to as elements of a set. These elements repeat in a predictable manner. It can be a template or model which can be used to generate things or parts of a thing, especially if the things that are created have enough in common for the underlying _____ to be inferred, in which case the things are said to exhibit the unique _____.
   a. 2-3 heap
   b. 120-cell
   c. 1-center problem
   d. Pattern

20. In general topology and related areas of mathematics, the _____ (inductive topology or strong topology) on a set X, with respect to a family of functions into X, is the finest topology on X which makes those functions continuous.

Given a set X and a family of topological spaces Y_i with functions

$$f_i : Y_i \to X$$

the _____ τ on X is the finest topology such that each

$$f_i : Y_i \to (X, \tau)$$

is continuous.

Explicitly, the _____ may be described as follows: a subset U of X is open if and only if $f_i^{-1}(U)$ is open in Y_i for each i ∈ I.

a. Wallman compactification
b. Cylinder set
c. Final topology
d. Gluing axiom

21. An _____ is an angle formed by one side of a simple polygon and a line extended from that side.
a. Interior angle
b. Exterior angle
c. Angular diameter
d. Orthogon

22. In geometry, an _____ is an angle formed by two sides of a simple polygon that share an endpoint, namely, the angle on the inner side of the polygon. A simple polygon has exactly one internal angle per vertex.

If every internal angle of a polygon is at most 180 degrees, the polygon is called convex.

a. Angle bisector
b. Interior angle
c. Exterior angle
d. Angle chasing

23. _____ are formed when a given transversal line crosses two coplanar lines. The _____ are not necessarily congruent. In the event that the _____ are congruent, these angles can be used to determine the degrees of the other angles of the parallel lines.
a. Brocard circle
b. Prismatic pentagonal tiling
c. Conformal connection
d. Corresponding Angles

24. In geometry a _____ is traditionally a plane figure that is bounded by a closed path or circuit, composed of a finite sequence of straight line segments. These segments are called its edges or sides, and the points where two edges meet are the _____'s vertices or corners. The interior of the _____ is sometimes called its body.
a. Regular polygon
b. Polygonal curve
c. Parallelogon
d. Polygon

25. _____ are used in computer graphics to compose images that are three-dimensional in appearance. Usually triangular, _____ arise when an object's surface is modeled, vertices are selected, and the object is rendered in a wire frame model. This is quicker to display than a shaded model; thus the _____ are a stage in computer animation.
a. Visibility polygon
b. Heptadecagon
c. Triskaidecagon
d. Polygons

26. In geometry, a _____ is a polygon with four sides or edges and four vertices or corners. Sometimes, the term quadrangle is used, for etymological symmetry with triangle, and sometimes tetragon for consistency with pentagon, hexagon and so on. The interior angles of a _____ add up to 360 degrees of arc.
- a. 2-3 heap
- b. 1-center problem
- c. 120-cell
- d. Quadrilateral

27. A _____ is a polygon which is equiangular and equilateral. _____s may be convex or star.

These properties apply to both convex and star _____s.

- a. Star-shaped polygon
- b. Regular decagon
- c. Constructible polygon
- d. Regular polygon

28. A _____ is one of the basic shapes of geometry: a polygon with three corners or vertices and three sides or edges which are line segments. A _____ with vertices A, B, and C is denoted ABC.

In Euclidean geometry any three non-collinear points determine a unique _____ and a unique plane.

- a. Kepler triangle
- b. 1-center problem
- c. Fuhrmann circle
- d. Triangle

29. In mathematics, the concept of a _____ tries to capture the intuitive idea of a geometrical one-dimensional and continuous object. A simple example is the circle. In everyday use of the term '_____', a straight line is not curved, but in mathematical parlance _____s include straight lines and line segments.
- a. Negative pedal curve
- b. Kappa curve
- c. Quadrifolium
- d. Curve

30. In geometry, an _____ is a triangle in which all three sides have equal lengths. In traditional or Euclidean geometry, _____s are also equiangular; that is, all three internal angles are also equal to each other and are each 60°. They are regular polygons, and can therefore also be referred to as regular triangles.
- a. A Mathematical Theory of Communication
- b. Isotomic conjugate
- c. A chemical equation
- d. Equilateral triangle

31. An _____ is a triangle that has one internal angle larger than 90°
- a. Isotomic conjugate
- b. A chemical equation
- c. A Mathematical Theory of Communication
- d. Obtuse triangle

32. In geometry, a _____ is a quadrilateral with two sets of parallel sides. The opposite sides of a _____ are of equal length, and the opposite angles of a _____ are congruent. The three-dimensional counterpart of a _____ is a parallelepiped.
- a. 1-center problem
- b. 120-cell
- c. 2-3 heap
- d. Parallelogram

33. In geometry, a _____ is defined as a quadrilateral where all four of its angles are right angles.

a. Point group in two dimensions
b. Polytope
c. Rectangle
d. Cantor-Dedekind axiom

34. In geometry, a _____ , or rhomb is an equilateral parallelogram. In other words, it is a four-sided polygon in which every side has the same length.

The _____ is often casually called a diamond, after the diamonds suit in playing cards, or a lozenge, because those shapes are rhombi, although rhombi are not necessarily diamonds or lozenges.

a. 2-3 heap
b. Rhombus
c. 1-center problem
d. 120-cell

35. _____ is a dissection puzzle consisting of 7 flat shapes called tans, which fit together to form a shape of some sort. The objective is to form a specific shape with seven pieces. The shape has to contain all the pieces, which must not overlap and touch each other.

a. 1-center problem
b. Tantrix
c. Tangram
d. Mutilated chessboard

36. A _____ or a trapezium is a quadrilateral that has at least one pair of parallel lines for sides.

Some authors define it as a quadrilateral having exactly one pair of parallel sides, so as to exclude parallelograms, which otherwise would be regarded as a special type of _____ , but most mathematicians use the inclusive definition.

In North America, the term trapezium is used to refer to a quadrilateral with no parallel sides.

a. Lozenge
b. Rhomboid
c. Trapezium
d. Trapezoid

37. A _____ is a software program that facilitates symbolic mathematics. The core functionality of a CAS is manipulation of mathematical expressions in symbolic form.

The symbolic manipulations supported typically include

- simplification to the smallest possible expression or some standard form, including automatic simplification with assumptions and simplification with constraints
- substitution of symbolic, functors or numeric values for expressions
- change of form of expressions: expanding products and powers, partial and full factorization, rewriting as partial fractions, constraint satisfaction, rewriting trigonometric functions as exponentials, etc.
- partial and total differentiation
- symbolic constrained and unconstrained global optimization
- solution of linear and some non-linear equations over various domains
- solution of some differential and difference equations
- taking some limits
- some indefinite and definite integration, including multidimensional integrals
- integral transforms
- arbitrary-precision numeric operations
- Series operations such as expansion, summation and products
- matrix operations including products, inverses, etc.
- display of mathematical expressions in two-dimensional mathematical form, often using typesetting systems similar to TeX
- add-ons for use in applied mathematics such as physics packages for physical computation
- plotting graphs and parametric plots of functions in two and three dimensions, and animating them
- APIs for linking it on an external program such as a database, or using in a programming language to use the _____
- drawing charts and diagrams
- string manipulation such as matching and searching
- statistical computation
- Theorem proving and verification
- graphic production and editing such as CGI and signal processing as image processing
- sound synthesis

Many also include a programming language, allowing users to implement their own algorithms.

Some _____s focus on a specific area of application; these are typically developed in academia and are free.

a. 120-cell
c. 2-3 heap
b. Computer algebra system
d. 1-center problem

38. _____ is a quantity expressing the two-dimensional size of a defined part of a surface, typically a region bounded by a closed curve. The term surface _____ refers to the total _____ of the exposed surface of a 3-dimensional solid, such as the sum of the _____s of the exposed sides of a polyhedron. _____ is an important invariant in the differential geometry of surfaces.

a. Area
b. A posteriori
c. A Mathematical Theory of Communication
d. A chemical equation

39. In mathematics the concept of a _____ generalizes notions such as 'length', 'area', and 'volume'. Informally, given some base set, a '_____' is any consistent assignment of 'sizes' to the subsets of the base set. Depending on the application, the 'size' of a subset may be interpreted as its physical size, the amount of something that lies within the subset, or the probability that some random process will yield a result within the subset.
   a. Cusp
   b. Measure
   c. Lattice
   d. Congruent

40. In classical geometry, a _____ of a circle or sphere is any line segment from its center to its boundary. By extension, the _____ of a circle or sphere is the length of any such segment. The _____ is half the diameter. In science and engineering the term _____ of curvature is commonly used as a synonym for _____.
   a. Non-Euclidean geometry
   b. Duoprism
   c. Birational geometry
   d. Radius

41. In trigonometry, the _____ is a function defined as tan x = $^{\sin x}/_{\cos x}$. The function is so-named because it can be defined as the length of a certain segment of a _____ (in the geometric sense) to the unit circle. In plane geometry, a line is _____ to a curve, at some point, if both line and curve pass through the point with the same direction.
   a. Tangent
   b. Conformal geometry
   c. Hopf conjectures
   d. Projective connection

42. A _____ is a simple shape of Euclidean geometry consisting of those points in a plane which are at a constant distance, called the radius, from a fixed point, called the center. A _____ with center A is sometimes denoted by the symbol A.

A chord of a _____ is a line segment whose two endpoints lie on the _____.

   a. Circular segment
   b. Circumcircle
   c. Malfatti circles
   d. Circle

43. _____ is a term in mathematics. It can refer to:

   • a _____ line, in geometry
   • the trigonometric function called _____
   • the _____ method, a root-finding algorithm in numerical analysis

   a. Solvable
   b. Large set
   c. Secant
   d. Separable

44. In mathematics, a _____ is a convincing demonstration that some mathematical statement is necessarily true. _____s are obtained from deductive reasoning, rather than from inductive or empirical arguments. That is, a _____ must demonstrate that a statement is true in all cases, without a single exception.

a. Congruent
b. Germ
c. Conchoid
d. Proof

45. In mathematics, a _____ is a statement that can be proved on the basis of explicitly stated or previously agreed assumptions.
    a. Logical value
    b. Theorem
    c. Disjunction introduction
    d. Boolean function

46. The _____ is πr^2 when the circle has radius r. Here the symbol π denotes, as usual, the constant ratio of the circumference of a circle to its diameter.

Modern mathematics can obtain the area using the methods of integral calculus or its more sophisticated offspring, real analysis.

   a. Ultraparallel theorem
   b. A chemical equation
   c. Area of a circle
   d. A Mathematical Theory of Communication

47. The _____ is the length of the line that bounds an area In the special case where the area is circular, the _____ is known as the circumference.
    a. Reflection symmetry
    b. Multilateration
    c. Concyclic
    d. Perimeter

48. In mathematics and in the sciences, a _____ (plural: _____e, formulæ or _____s) is a concise way of expressing information symbolically (as in a mathematical or chemical _____), or a general relationship between quantities. One of many famous _____e is Albert Einstein's $E = mc^2$ (see special relativity

In mathematics, a _____ is a key to solve an equation with variables. For example, the problem of determining the volume of a sphere is one that requires a significant amount of integral calculus to solve.

   a. 120-cell
   b. 2-3 heap
   c. 1-center problem
   d. Formula

49. _____ is a general term for any type of information processing. This includes phenomena ranging from human thinking to calculations with a more narrow meaning. _____ is a process following a well-defined model that is understood and can be expressed in an algorithm, protocol, network topology, etc.
    a. 120-cell
    b. 2-3 heap
    c. 1-center problem
    d. Computation

50. In geometry, two sets of points are called _____ if one can be transformed into the other by an isometry. Less formally, two figures are _____ if they have the same shape and size, but are in different positions.

In a Euclidean system, congruence is fundamental; it is the counterpart of equality for numbers.

   a. Germ
   b. Function
   c. Gamma test
   d. Congruent

51. _____ refers to any mathematics of the peoples of Mesopotamia, from the days of the early Sumerians to the fall of Babylon in 539 BC. In contrast to the scarcity of sources in Egyptian mathematics, our knowledge of _____ is derived from some 400 clay tablets unearthed since the 1850s. Written in Cuneiform script, tablets were inscribed while the clay was moist, and baked hard in an oven or by the heat of the sun.

a. 120-cell
b. 1-center problem
c. 2-3 heap
d. Babylonian mathematics

52. As an abstract term, _____ means similarity between objects.

a. 120-cell
b. 1-center problem
c. 2-3 heap
d. Congruence

53. In linear algebra, two n-by-n matrices A and B over the field K are called _____ if there exists an invertible n-by-n matrix P over K such that

$$P^{-1}AP = B.$$

One of the meanings of the term similarity transformation is such a transformation of a matrix A into a matrix B.

Similarity is an equivalence relation on the space of square matrices.

_____ matrices share many properties:

- rank
- determinant
- trace
- eigenvalues
- characteristic polynomial
- minimal polynomial
- elementary divisors

There are two reasons for these facts:

- two _____ matrices can be thought of as describing the same linear map, but with respect to different bases
- the map $X \mapsto P^{-1}XP$ is an automorphism of the associative algebra of all n-by-n matrices, as the one-object case of the above category of all matrices.

Because of this, for a given matrix A, one is interested in finding a simple 'normal form' B which is _____ to A -- the study of A then reduces to the study of the simpler matrix B.

a. Dense
b. Blinding
c. Coherence
d. Similar

Chapter 9. Geometry

54. A _____ is the longest side of a right triangle, the side opposite of the right angle. The length of the _____ of a right triangle can be found using the Pythagorean theorem, which states that the square of the length of the _____ equals the sum of the squares of the lengths of the two other sides.

For example, if one of the other sides has a length of 3 meters and the other has a length of 4 m.

a. Golden angle
b. Reflection symmetry
c. Concyclic points
d. Hypotenuse

55. In mathematics, the _____ or Pythagoras' theorem is a relation in Euclidean geometry among the three sides of a right triangle. The theorem is named after the Greek mathematician Pythagoras, who by tradition is credited with its discovery and proof, although it is often argued that knowledge of the theory predates him.. The theorem is as follows:

In any right triangle, the area of the square whose side is the hypotenuse is equal to the sum of the areas of the squares whose sides are the two legs.

a. 2-3 heap
b. Pythagorean theorem
c. 1-center problem
d. 120-cell

56. A _____ consists of three positive integers a, b, and c, such that $a^2 + b^2 = c^2$. Such a triple is commonly written, and a well-known example is. If is a _____, then so is for any positive integer k.

a. 1-center problem
b. 2-3 heap
c. 120-cell
d. Pythagorean triple

57. A _____ is any polyhedron with twelve faces, but usually a regular _____ is meant: a Platonic solid composed of twelve regular pentagonal faces, with three meeting at each vertex. It has twenty vertices and thirty edges. Its dual polyhedron is the icosahedron.

a. 1-center problem
b. 2-3 heap
c. 120-cell
d. Dodecahedron

58. In modern mathematical language, distance and angle can be generalized easily to 4-dimensional, 5-dimensional, and even higher-dimensional spaces. An n-dimensional space with notions of distance and angle that obey the Euclidean relationships is called an n-dimensional _____

a. Euclidean space
b. Orthant
c. Equal incircles theorem
d. Orthographic projection

59. A _____ is a polyhedron with six faces. A regular _____, with all its faces square, is a cube.

There many kinds of _____, some topologically similar to the cube, and some not.

a. Hoberman sphere
b. Wythoff construction
c. Parallelepiped
d. Hexahedron

60. In geometry, an _____ is any polyhedron having 20 faces, but usually a regular _____ is implied, which has equilateral triangles as faces.

The regular _____ is one of the five Platonic solids. It is a convex regular polyhedron composed of twenty triangular faces, with five meeting at each of the twelve vertices.

- a. A chemical equation
- b. A Mathematical Theory of Communication
- c. A posteriori
- d. Icosahedron

61. An _____ is a polyhedron with eight faces. A regular _____ is a Platonic solid composed of eight equilateral triangles, four of which meet at each vertex.

The _____'s symmetry group is O_h, of order 48.

- a. A Mathematical Theory of Communication
- b. Octahedron
- c. A posteriori
- d. A chemical equation

62. A _____ is often defined as a geometric object with flat faces and straight edges .

This definition of a _____ is not very precise, and to a modern mathematician is quite unsatisfactory. Grünbaum observed that:

The Original Sin in the theory of polyhedra goes back to Euclid, and through Kepler, Poinsot, Cauchy and many others ...

- a. 2-3 heap
- b. 120-cell
- c. Polyhedron
- d. 1-center problem

63. A _____ is a polyhedron composed of four triangular faces, three of which meet at each vertex. A regular _____ is one in which the four triangles are regular, or 'equilateral', and is one of the Platonic solids.

The _____ is one kind of pyramid, which is a polyhedron with a flat polygon base and triangular faces connecting the base to a common point.

- a. 120-cell
- b. 1-center problem
- c. 2-3 heap
- d. Tetrahedron

64. In geometry, a _____ is a three-dimensional figure formed by six parallelograms. It is to a parallelogram as a cube is to a square: Euclidean geometry supports all four notions but affine geometry admits only parallelograms and _____s. Three equivalent definitions of _____ are

- a polyhedron with six faces, each of which is a parallelogram,
- a hexahedron with three pairs of parallel faces.
- a prism of which the base is a parallelogram,

The cuboid, cube, and the rhombohedron are all specific cases of _____.

_____s are a subclass of the prismatoids.

a. Hoberman sphere
b. Polyhedral compound
c. Wythoff construction
d. Parallelepiped

65. A _____ is a building where the upper surfaces are triangular and converge on one point. The base of _____s are usually quadrilateral or trilateral, meaning that a _____ usually has four or five faces. A _____'s design, with the majority of the weight closer to the ground, means that less material higher up on the _____ will be pushing down from above.

a. 1-center problem
b. 2-3 heap
c. 120-cell
d. Pyramid

66. _____ is a three-dimensional geometric shape formed by straight lines through a fixed point vertex to the points of a fixed curve directrix.

a. 120-cell
b. Right circular cone
c. 2-3 heap
d. 1-center problem

67. In common usage, a cylinder is taken to mean a finite section of a _____ with its ends closed to form two circular surfaces, as in the figure (right.) If the cylinder has a radius r and length (height) h, then its volume is given by

$$V = \pi r^2 h$$

and its surface area is:

- the area of the top (πr^2) +
- the area of the bottom (πr^2) +
- the area of the side $(2\pi r h)$.

Therefore without the top or bottom (lateral area), the surface area is

$$A = 2\pi r h.$$

With the top and bottom, the surface area is

$$A = 2\pi r^2 + 2\pi r h = 2\pi r(r + h).$$

For a given volume, the cylinder with the smallest surface area has h = 2r. For a given surface area, the cylinder with the largest volume has h = 2r, i.e. the cylinder fits in a cube (height = diameter.)

Cylindric sections are the intersections of cylinders with planes.

a. 1-center problem
b. 2-3 heap
c. 120-cell
d. Right circular cylinder

68. In mathematics, specifically in topology, a _____ is a two-dimensional manifold. The most familiar examples are those that arise as the boundaries of solid objects in ordinary three-dimensional Euclidean space, EÂ³. On the other hand, there are also more exotic _____s, that are so 'contorted' that they cannot be embedded in three-dimensional space at all.
   a. Standard torus
   b. Homoeoid
   c. Cross-cap
   d. Surface

69. _____ is how much exposed area an object has. It is expressed in square units. If an object has flat faces, its _____ can be calculated by adding together the areas of its faces.
   a. Reflection group
   b. Compactness measure of a shape
   c. Relative dimension
   d. Surface area

70. In geometry, a _____ is a surface of revolution generated by revolving a circle in three dimensional space about an axis coplanar with the circle, which does not touch the circle. Examples of tori include the surfaces of doughnuts and inner tubes. The solid contained by the surface is known as a toroid.
   a. Spheroid
   b. Torus
   c. Focal surface
   d. PDE surfaces

71. In mathematics, the _____s are analogs of the ordinary trigonometric functions. The basic _____s are the hyperbolic sine 'sinh', and the hyperbolic cosine 'cosh', from which are derived the hyperbolic tangent 'tanh', etc., in analogy to the derived trigonometric functions. The inverse _____ are the area hyperbolic sine 'arsinh' (also called 'asinh', or sometimes by the misnomer of 'arcsinh') and so on.
   a. Hyperbolic function
   b. Rectangular function
   c. Square root
   d. Heaviside step function

72. In common usage, a cylinder is taken to mean a finite section of a right _____ with its ends closed to form two circular surfaces, as in the figure (right.) If the cylinder has a radius r and length (height) h, then its volume is given by

$$V = \pi r^2 h$$

and its surface area is:

- the area of the top (πr^2) +
- the area of the bottom (πr^2) +
- the area of the side $(2\pi r h)$.

Therefore without the top or bottom (lateral area), the surface area is

$$A = 2\pi r h.$$

With the top and bottom, the surface area is

$$A = 2\pi r^2 + 2\pi rh = 2\pi r(r+h).$$

For a given volume, the cylinder with the smallest surface area has h = 2r. For a given surface area, the cylinder with the largest volume has h = 2r, i.e. the cylinder fits in a cube (height = diameter.)

Cylindric sections are the intersections of cylinders with planes.

- a. 120-cell
- c. 2-3 heap
- b. 1-center problem
- d. Circular cylinder

73. A _____ is a three-dimensional geometric shape that tapers smoothly from a flat, round base to a point called the apex or vertex. More precisely, it is the solid figure bounded by a plane base and the surface formed by the locus of all straight line segments joining the apex to the perimeter of the base. The term '_____' sometimes refers just to the surface of this solid figure, or just to the lateral surface.
- a. Blocking
- c. Cone
- b. Characteristic
- d. Gravity waves

74. In mathematics, a _____ is a quadric surface, with the following equation in Cartesian coordinates: $(x/a)^2 + (y/b)^2 = 1$.
- a. Derivative algebra
- c. Discontinuity
- b. Free
- d. Cylinder

75. The _____ of any solid, plasma, vacuum or theoretical object is how much three-dimensional space it occupies, often quantified numerically. One-dimensional figures and two-dimensional shapes are assigned zero _____ in the three-dimensional space. _____ is presented as ml or cm^3.

_____s of straight-edged and circular shapes are calculated using arithmetic formulae.

- a. Cauchy momentum equation
- c. Thermodynamic limit
- b. Stress-energy tensor
- d. Volume

76. A _____ is a symmetrical geometrical object. In non-mathematical usage, the term is used to refer either to a round ball or to its two-dimensional surface. In mathematics, a _____ is the set of all points in three-dimensional space which are at distance r from a fixed point of that space, where r is a positive real number called the radius of the _____.
- a. Lie derivative
- c. Differential geometry of curves
- b. Sphere
- d. Differentiable manifold

77. In geometry, a _____ is a type of isometry of the Euclidean plane: the combination of a reflection in a line and a translation along that line. Reversing the order of combining gives the same result. Depending on context, we may consider a reflection a special case, where the translation vector is the zero vector.

Chapter 9. Geometry

a. Hubbard-Stratonovich transformation
b. Surjective
c. Glide Reflection
d. Rotation of axes

78. An _____ is an artifact, usually two-dimensional (a picture), that has a similar appearance to some subject--usually a physical object or a person.

_____s may be two-dimensional, such as a photograph, screen display, and as well as a three-dimensional, such as a statue. They may be captured by optical devices--such as cameras, mirrors, lenses, telescopes, microscopes, etc.

a. A chemical equation
b. A posteriori
c. A Mathematical Theory of Communication
d. Image

79. _____ generally conveys two primary meanings. The first is an imprecise sense of harmonious or aesthetically-pleasing proportionality and balance; such that it reflects beauty or perfection. The second meaning is a precise and well-defined concept of balance or 'patterned self-similarity' that can be demonstrated or proved according to the rules of a formal system: by geometry, through physics or otherwise.

a. Symmetry breaking
b. Molecular symmetry
c. Symmetry
d. Tessellation

80. _____ is the interpreting of the meaning of a text and the subsequent production of an equivalent text, likewise called a '_____,' that communicates the same message in another language. The text to be translated is called the 'source text,' and the language that it is to be translated into is called the 'target language'; the final product is sometimes called the 'target text.'

_____ must take into account constraints that include context, the rules of grammar of the two languages, their writing conventions, and their idioms. A common misconception is that there exists a simple word-for-word correspondence between any two languages, and that _____ is a straightforward mechanical process; such a word-for-word _____, however, cannot take into account context, grammar, conventions, and idioms.

a. 1-center problem
b. 2-3 heap
c. 120-cell
d. Translation

81. The term _____ or centre is used in various contexts in abstract algebra to denote the set of all those elements that commute with all other elements. More specifically:

- The _____ of a group G consists of all those elements x in G such that xg = gx for all g in G. This is a normal subgroup of G.
- The _____ of a ring R is the subset of R consisting of all those elements x of R such that xr = rx for all r in R. The _____ is a commutative subring of R, so R is an algebra over its _____.
- The _____ of an algebra A consists of all those elements x of A such that xa = ax for all a in A. See also: central simple algebra.
- The _____ of a Lie algebra L consists of all those elements x in L such that [x,a] = 0 for all a in L. This is an ideal of the Lie algebra L.
- The _____ of a monoidal category C consists of pairs *a natural isomorphism satisfying certain axioms*.

a. Block size
b. Disk
c. Brute Force
d. Center

82. In mathematics, the term _____ has several different important meanings:

- An _____ is an equality that remains true regardless of the values of any variables that appear within it, to distinguish it from an equality which is true under more particular conditions. For this, the 'triple bar' symbol ≡ is sometimes used.
- In algebra, an _____ or _____ element of a set S with a binary operation Â· is an element e that, when combined with any element x of S, produces that same x. That is, eÂ·x = xÂ·e = x for all x in S.
    - The _____ function from a set S to itself, often denoted id or id_S, s the function such that i = x for all x in S. This function serves as the _____ element in the set of all functions from S to itself with respect to function composition.
    - In linear algebra, the _____ matrix of size n is the n-by-n square matrix with ones on the main diagonal and zeros elsewhere. This matrix serves as the _____ with respect to matrix multiplication.

A common example of the first meaning is the trigonometric _____

$$\sin^2 \theta + \cos^2 \theta = 1$$

which is true for all real values of θ, as opposed to

$$\cos \theta = 1,$$

which is true only for some values of θ, not all. For example, the latter equation is true when $\theta = 0$, false when $\theta = 2$

Chapter 9. Geometry

The concepts of 'additive _____' and 'multiplicative _____' are central to the Peano axioms. The number 0 is the 'additive _____' for integers, real numbers, and complex numbers. For the real numbers, for all $a \in \mathbb{R}$,

$$0 + a = a,$$

$$a + 0 = a, \text{ and}$$

$$0 + 0 = 0.$$

Similarly, The number 1 is the 'multiplicative _____' for integers, real numbers, and complex numbers.

- a. Action
- b. Intersection
- c. Identity
- d. ARIA

83. A _____ or tiling of the plane is a collection of plane figures that fills the plane with no overlaps and no gaps. One may also speak of _____s of the parts of the plane or of other surfaces. Generalizations to higher dimensions are also possible.
- a. Symmetry breaking
- b. Directional symmetry
- c. Tessellation
- d. Molecular symmetry

84. In traditional logic, an _____ or postulate is a proposition that is not proved or demonstrated but considered to be either self-evident, or subject to necessary decision. Therefore, its truth is taken for granted, and serves as a starting point for deducing and inferring other truths.

In mathematics, the term _____ is used in two related but distinguishable senses: 'logical _____s' and 'non-logical _____s'.

- a. Algebraic logic
- b. AND-OR-Invert
- c. Enumerative definition
- d. Axiom

85. In mathematics, an _____ or member of a set is any one of the distinct objects that make up that set.

Writing A = {1,2,3,4}, means that the _____s of the set A are the numbers 1, 2, 3 and 4. Groups of _____s of A, for example {1,2}, are subsets of A.

- a. Universal code
- b. Order
- c. Ideal
- d. Element

86. _____ is a mathematical system attributed to the Greek mathematician Euclid of Alexandria. Euclid's Elements is the earliest known systematic discussion of geometry. It has been one of the most influential books in history, as much for its method as for its mathematical content.

Chapter 9. Geometry

a. Euclidean geometry
c. Analytic geometry
b. Infinitely near point
d. Equidimensional

87. _____ Galilei (15 February 1564 - 8 January 1642) was a Tuscan physicist, mathematician, astronomer, and philosopher who played a major role in the Scientific Revolution. His achievements include improvements to the telescope and consequent astronomical observations, and support for Copernicanism. _____ has been called the 'father of modern observational astronomy', the 'father of modern physics', the 'father of science', and 'the Father of Modern Science.' The motion of uniformly accelerated objects, taught in nearly all high school and introductory college physics courses, was studied by _____ as the subject of kinematics.

a. Francesco Severi
c. Galileo
b. David Naccache
d. Jan Kowalewski

88. In mathematics, _____ describes hyperbolic and elliptic geometry, which are contrasted with Euclidean geometry. The essential difference between Euclidean and _____ is the nature of parallel lines. Euclid's fifth postulate, the parallel postulate, is equivalent to Playfair's postulate, which states that, within a two-dimensional plane, for any given line l and a point A, which is not on l, there is exactly one line through A that does not intersect l.

a. Nash function
c. Tropical geometry
b. Brascamp-Lieb inequality
d. Non-Euclidean geometry

89. In mathematics, the _____ of a Euclidean space is a special point, usually denoted by the letter O, used as a fixed point of reference for the geometry of the surrounding space. In a Cartesian coordinate system, the _____ is the point where the axes of the system intersect. In Euclidean geometry, the _____ may be chosen freely as any convenient point of reference.

a. Interval
c. OMAC
b. Autonomous system
d. Origin

90. In the mathematical field of descriptive set theory, a subset A of a Polish space X is _____ if it is Σ^1_n for some positive integer n. Here A is

- Σ^1_1 if A is analytic
- Π^1_n if the complement of A, $X \setminus A$, is Σ^1_n
- Σ^1_{n+1} if there is a Polish space Y and a Π^1_n subset $C \subseteq X \times Y$ such that A is the projection of C; that is, $A = \{x \in X | (\exists y \in Y) \langle x, y \rangle \in C\}$

The choice of the Polish space Y in the third clause above is not very important; it could be replaced in the definition by a fixed uncountable Polish space, say Baire space or Cantor space or the real line.

There is a close relationship between the relativized analytical hierarchy on subsets of Baire space and the _____ hierarchy on subsets of Baire space. Not every Σ^1_n subset of Baire space is Σ^1_n.

a. Character
c. Forcing
b. Bounded
d. Projective

Chapter 9. Geometry

91. _____ is a non-metrical form of geometry, notable for its principle of duality. _____ grew out of the principles of perspective art established during the Renaissance period, and was first systematically developed by Desargues in the 17th century, although it did not achieve prominence as a field of mathematics until the early 19th century through the work of Poncelet and others. _____ involves affine, metrical, and Euclidean geometries as its special and more restrictive cases.

   a. Projective geometry
   b. Non-Euclidean geometry
   c. Corresponding sides
   d. Transformation geometry

92. In geometry, a _____ of radius R is a surface of curvature $-1/R^2$, by analogy with the sphere of radius R, which is a surface of curvature $1/R^2$. The term was introduced by Eugenio Beltrami in his 1868 paper on models of hyperbolic geometry.

The term is also used to refer to what is traditionally called a tractricoid: the result of revolving a tractrix about its asymptote, which is the subject of

It is a singular space, but away from the singularities, it has constant negative Gaussian curvature and therefore is locally isometric to a hyperbolic plane.

   a. Systolic freedom
   b. Pseudosphere
   c. Round function
   d. Tangent

93. Georg Friedrich Bernhard _____ was a German mathematician who made important contributions to analysis and differential geometry, some of them paving the way for the later development of general relativity.

_____ was born in Breselenz, a village near Dannenberg in the Kingdom of Hanover in what is today Germany. His father, Friedrich Bernhard _____, was a poor Lutheran pastor in Breselenz who fought in the Napoleonic Wars.

   a. Brook Taylor
   b. Paul C. van Oorschot
   c. Gustave Bertrand
   d. Riemann

94. _____ is the curve along which a small object moves, under the influence of friction, when pulled on a horizontal plane by a piece of thread and a puller that moves at a right angle to the initial line between the object and the puller at an infinitesimal speed. It is therefore a curve of pursuit. It was first introduced by Claude Perrault in 1670, and later studied by Sir Isaac Newton and Christian Huygen.

   a. Folium of Descartes
   b. Sinusoidal spiral
   c. Cycloid
   d. Tractrix

95. _____ is the branch of mathematics that studies the properties of a space that are preserved under continuous deformations. _____ grew out of geometry, but unlike geometry, _____ is not concerned with metric properties such as distances between points. Instead, _____ involves the study of properties that describe how a space is assembled, such as connectedness and orientability.

   a. 1-center problem
   b. Topology
   c. Structure
   d. Ring

Chapter 9. Geometry

96. In mathematics, the _____ is a certain non-orientable surface, i.e., a surface with no distinct 'inner' and 'outer' sides. Other related non-orientable objects include the Möbius strip and the real projective plane. Whereas a Möbius strip is a two dimensional surface with boundary, a _____ has no boundary.
   a. 120-cell
   b. Klein bottle
   c. 2-3 heap
   d. 1-center problem

97. _____ was a German mathematician, known for his work in group theory, function theory, non-Euclidean geometry, and on the connections between geometry and group theory. His 1872 Erlangen Program, classifying geometries by their underlying symmetry groups, was a hugely influential synthesis of much of the mathematics of the day.

Klein was born in Düsseldorf, to Prussian parents; his father was a Prussian government official stationed in the Rhine Province.

   a. Motoo Kimura
   b. Kazushige GotÅ
   c. Friedrich Wilhelm Bessel
   d. Felix Christian Klein

98. A _____ is a structure built to span a gorge, valley, road, railroad track, river, body of water for the purpose of providing passage over the obstacle. Designs of _____s will vary depending on the function of the _____ and the nature of the terrain where the _____ is to be constructed. Roman _____ of Córdoba, Spain, built in the 1st century BC. Ponte di Pietra in Verona, Italy. A log _____ in the French Alps near Vallorcine. An English 18th century example of a _____ in the Palladian style, with shops on the span: Pulteney _____, Bath A Han Dynasty Chinese miniature model of two residential towers joined by a _____

The first _____s were made by nature -- as simple as a log fallen across a stream.

   a. 2-3 heap
   b. 1-center problem
   c. 120-cell
   d. Bridge

99. In mathematics and computer science, _____ is the study of graphs: mathematical structures used to model pairwise relations between objects from a certain collection. A 'graph' in this context refers to a collection of vertices or 'nodes' and a collection of edges that connect pairs of vertices. A graph may be undirected, meaning that there is no distinction between the two vertices associated with each edge, or its edges may be directed from one vertex to another; see graph for more detailed definitions and for other variations in the types of graphs that are commonly considered.
   a. Pooling design
   b. Graph theory
   c. Discrete mathematics
   d. Partial equivalence relation

100. In graph theory, a _____ is a digraph with weighted edges. These _____s have become an especially useful concept in analysing the interaction between biology and mathematics. Using _____s of all types; various applications based on the creativity of the mathematician along with their environment can be evaluated in all sorts of manners.
   a. Chord
   b. Copula
   c. Colossus
   d. Network

Chapter 9. Geometry

101. The word _____ has many distinct meanings in different fields of knowledge, depending on their methodologies and the context of discussion. Broadly speaking we can say that a _____ is some kind of belief or claim that (supposedly) explains, asserts, or consolidates some class of claims. Additionally, in contrast with a theorem the statement of the _____ is generally accepted only in some tentative fashion as opposed to regarding it as having been conclusively established.

  a. Defined
  b. Theory
  c. Transport of structure
  d. Per mil

102. _____ is the likelihood or chance that something is the case or will happen. Theoretical _____ is used extensively in areas such as statistics, mathematics, science and philosophy to draw conclusions about the likelihood of potential events and the underlying mechanics of complex systems.

The word _____ does not have a consistent direct definition.

  a. Probability
  b. Statistical significance
  c. Discrete random variable
  d. Standardized moment

103. A _____ is generally 'a rough or fragmented geometric shape that can be split into parts, each of which is a reduced-size copy of the whole,' a property called self-similarity. The term was coined by Benoît Mandelbrot in 1975 and was derived from the Latin fractus meaning 'broken' or 'fractured.' A mathematical _____ is based on an equation that undergoes iteration, a form of feedback based on recursion.

A _____ often has the following features:

- It has a fine structure at arbitrarily small scales.
- It is too irregular to be easily described in traditional Euclidean geometric language.
- It is self-similar.
- It has a Hausdorff dimension which is greater than its topological dimension.
- It has a simple and recursive definition.

Because they appear similar at all levels of magnification, _____s are often considered to be infinitely complex. Natural objects that approximate _____s to a degree include clouds, mountain ranges, lightning bolts, coastlines, and snow flakes.

  a. Cube
  b. Fractal
  c. Zero-point energy
  d. Logical disjunction

Chapter 10. Trigonometry

1. _____ refers to any mathematics of the peoples of Mesopotamia, from the days of the early Sumerians to the fall of Babylon in 539 BC. In contrast to the scarcity of sources in Egyptian mathematics, our knowledge of _____ is derived from some 400 clay tablets unearthed since the 1850s. Written in Cuneiform script, tablets were inscribed while the clay was moist, and baked hard in an oven or by the heat of the sun.

   a. 1-center problem
   b. 120-cell
   c. 2-3 heap
   d. Babylonian mathematics

2. _____ (22 July 1784 - 17 March 1846) was a German mathematician, astronomer, and systematizer of the Bessel functions (which were discovered by Daniel Bernoulli.) He was a contemporary of Carl Gauss, also a mathematician and astronomer. The asteroid 1552 Bessel was named in his honour.

   a. Friedrich Wilhelm Bessel
   b. Raymond Merrill Smullyan
   c. Johann Bernoulli
   d. Paul C. van Oorschot

3. _____, as that term is used in this article, is the mathematics written in Greek, developed from the 6th century BC to the 5th century AD around the Eastern shores of the Mediterranean. The word 'mathematics' itself derives from the ancient Greek μαθημα, meaning 'subject of instruction'.. The study of mathematics for its own sake and the use of generalized mathematical theories and proofs is the key difference between _____ and those of preceding civilizations.

   a. 120-cell
   b. Greek mathematics
   c. 1-center problem
   d. 2-3 heap

4. _____ is a branch of mathematics that deals with triangles, particularly those plane triangles in which one angle has 90 degrees. _____ deals with relationships between the sides and the angles of triangles and with the trigonometric functions, which describe those relationships.

_____ has applications in both pure mathematics and in applied mathematics, where it is essential in many branches of science and technology.

   a. Law of sines
   b. Sine
   c. Trigonometric functions
   d. Trigonometry

5. In geometry and trigonometry, an _____ is the figure formed by two rays sharing a common endpoint, called the vertex of the _____. The magnitude of the _____ is the 'amount of rotation' that separates the two rays, and can be measured by considering the length of circular arc swept out when one ray is rotated about the vertex to coincide with the other. Where there is no possibility of confusion, the term '_____' is used interchangeably for both the geometric configuration itself and for its angular magnitude.

   a. A posteriori
   b. A Mathematical Theory of Communication
   c. A chemical equation
   d. Angle

6. _____ is the title of a short book on logic by Gottlob Frege, published in 1879, and is also the name of the formal system set out in that book.

_____ is usually translated as concept writing or concept notation; the full title of the book identifies it as 'a formula language, modelled on that of arithmetic, of pure thought.' The _____ was arguably the most important publication in logic since Aristotle founded the subject. Frege's motivation for developing his formal approach to logic resembled Leibniz's motivation for his calculus ratiocinator.

a. 120-cell
b. 2-3 heap
c. 1-center problem
d. Begriffsschrift

7. In mathematics the concept of a _____ generalizes notions such as 'length', 'area', and 'volume'. Informally, given some base set, a '_____' is any consistent assignment of 'sizes' to the subsets of the base set. Depending on the application, the 'size' of a subset may be interpreted as its physical size, the amount of something that lies within the subset, or the probability that some random process will yield a result within the subset.
  a. Congruent
  b. Cusp
  c. Lattice
  d. Measure

8. In geometry, a _____ is a special kind of point, usually a corner of a polygon, polyhedron, or higher dimensional polytope. In the geometry of curves a _____ is a point of where the first derivative of curvature is zero. In graph theory, a _____ is the fundamental unit out of which graphs are formed
  a. Crib
  b. Duality
  c. Dini
  d. Vertex

9. _____ is the study of terms and their use. Terms are words and compound words that are used in specific contexts. Not to be confused with 'terms' in colloquial usages, the shortened form of technical terms which are defined within a discipline or specialty field.
  a. 2-3 heap
  b. 120-cell
  c. 1-center problem
  d. Terminology

10. An angle smaller than a right angle is called an _____ (less than 90 degrees).
  a. Euclidean geometry
  b. Acute angle
  c. Integral geometry
  d. Ultraparallel theorem

11. In geometry and trigonometry, a _____ is defined as an angle between two straight intersecting lines of ninety degrees, or one-quarter of a circle.
  a. Sine integral
  b. Trigonometry
  c. Right angle
  d. Trigonometric functions

12. An angle equal to two right angles is called a _____ (equal to 180 degrees).
  a. Theorem
  b. Straight angle
  c. Householder transformation
  d. Loomis-Whitney inequality

13. A pair of angles is _____ if their measurements add up to 180 degrees. If the two _____ angles are adjacent their non-shared sides form a straight line. The supplement of 135 would be 45.
  a. Supplementary
  b. FISH
  c. Cylinder
  d. Dense

14. A pair of angles are complementary if the sum of their measures add up to 90 degrees.

If the two _____ are adjacent (i.e. have a common vertex and share a side, but do not have any interior points in common) their non-shared sides form a right angle.

Chapter 10. Trigonometry

In Euclidean geometry, the two acute angles in a right triangle are complementary, because there are 180>° in a triangle and 90>° have been accounted for by the right angle.

- a. Hypotenuse
- b. Complementary Angles
- c. Quincunx
- d. Conway polyhedron notation

15. Initial objects are also called _____, and terminal objects are also called final.
    - a. Colimit
    - b. Terminal object
    - c. Direct limit
    - d. Coterminal

16. In algebraic geometry, _____ is a notion of genericity for a set of points, or other geometric objects. It means the general case situation, as opposed to some more special or coincidental cases that are possible. Its precise meaning differs in different settings.
    - a. Compactness measure of a shape
    - b. General position
    - c. Convexity
    - d. Lipschitz domain

17. In trigonometry, the _____ is a function defined as $\tan x = \sin x / \cos x$. The function is so-named because it can be defined as the length of a certain segment of a _____ (in the geometric sense) to the unit circle. In plane geometry, a line is _____ to a curve, at some point, if both line and curve pass through the point with the same direction.
    - a. Projective connection
    - b. Conformal geometry
    - c. Hopf conjectures
    - d. Tangent

18. In mathematics, the _____ functions are functions of an angle; they are important when studying triangles and modeling periodic phenomena, among many other applications.
    - a. Law of sines
    - b. Gudermannian function
    - c. Trigonometric
    - d. Coversine

19. In mathematics, the _____ are functions of an angle. They are important in the study of triangles and modeling periodic phenomena, among many other applications. _____ are commonly defined as ratios of two sides of a right triangle containing the angle, and can equivalently be defined as the lengths of various line segments from a unit circle.
    - a. Sine
    - b. Trigonometric integrals
    - c. Law of sines
    - d. Trigonometric functions

20. The mathematical concept of a _____ expresses the intuitive idea of deterministic dependence between two quantities, one of which is viewed as primary and the other as secondary. A _____ then is a way to associate a unique output for each input of a specified type, for example, a real number or an element of a given set.
    - a. Coherent
    - b. Function
    - c. Going up
    - d. Grill

21. In mathematics, the multiplicative inverse of a number x, denoted 1/x or x^{-1}, is the number which, when multiplied by x, yields 1. The multiplicative inverse of x is also called the _____ of x.
    - a. 1-center problem
    - b. 120-cell
    - c. Reciprocal
    - d. 2-3 heap

22. In mathematics, _____ are equalities that involve trigonometric functions that are true for every single value of the occurring variables. These identities are useful whenever expressions involving trigonometric functions need to be simplified. An important application is the integration of non-trigonometric functions: a common trick involves first using the substitution rule with a trigonometric function, and then simplifying the resulting integral with a trigonometric identity.
   a. Trigonometric identities
   b. 120-cell
   c. 1-center problem
   d. 2-3 heap

23. In mathematics, a function f is _____ of a function g if f whenever A and B are complementary angles. This definition typically applies to trigonometric functions.
   a. Balian-Low theorem
   b. Boxcar function
   c. Cofunction
   d. Birkhoff interpolation

24. In mathematics, a _____ is the end result of a division problem. It can also be expressed as the number of times the divisor divides into the dividend.
   a. Notation
   b. Limiting
   c. Marginal cost
   d. Quotient

25. A _____ is a software program that facilitates symbolic mathematics. The core functionality of a CAS is manipulation of mathematical expressions in symbolic form.

The symbolic manipulations supported typically include

- simplification to the smallest possible expression or some standard form, including automatic simplification with assumptions and simplification with constraints
- substitution of symbolic, functors or numeric values for expressions
- change of form of expressions: expanding products and powers, partial and full factorization, rewriting as partial fractions, constraint satisfaction, rewriting trigonometric functions as exponentials, etc.
- partial and total differentiation
- symbolic constrained and unconstrained global optimization
- solution of linear and some non-linear equations over various domains
- solution of some differential and difference equations
- taking some limits
- some indefinite and definite integration, including multidimensional integrals
- integral transforms
- arbitrary-precision numeric operations
- Series operations such as expansion, summation and products
- matrix operations including products, inverses, etc.
- display of mathematical expressions in two-dimensional mathematical form, often using typesetting systems similar to TeX
- add-ons for use in applied mathematics such as physics packages for physical computation
- plotting graphs and parametric plots of functions in two and three dimensions, and animating them
- APIs for linking it on an external program such as a database, or using in a programming language to use the _____
- drawing charts and diagrams
- string manipulation such as matching and searching
- statistical computation
- Theorem proving and verification
- graphic production and editing such as CGI and signal processing as image processing
- sound synthesis

Many also include a programming language, allowing users to implement their own algorithms.

Some _____s focus on a specific area of application; these are typically developed in academia and are free.

a. 2-3 heap
c. Computer algebra system

b. 1-center problem
d. 120-cell

26. A _____ is one of the basic shapes of geometry: a polygon with three corners or vertices and three sides or edges which are line segments. A _____ with vertices A, B, and C is denoted ABC.

In Euclidean geometry any three non-collinear points determine a unique _____ and a unique plane.

a. Fuhrmann circle
c. 1-center problem

b. Kepler triangle
d. Triangle

27. The _____ is a palimpsest on parchment in the form of a codex which originally was a copy of an otherwise unknown work of the ancient mathematician, physicist, and engineer Archimedes of Syracuse and other authors. Archimedes lived in the third century BC, but the copy was made in the tenth century AD by an anonymous scribe. In the twelfth century the codex was unbound and washed, in order that the parchment leaves could be folded in half and reused for a Christian liturgical text.

a. Archimedes Palimpsest
c. A posteriori

b. A chemical equation
d. A Mathematical Theory of Communication

28. A _____ typically refers to a class of handheld calculators that are capable of plotting graphs, solving simultaneous equations, and performing numerous other tasks with variables. Most popular _____s are also programmable, allowing the user to create customized programs, typically for scientific/engineering and education applications. Due to their large displays intended for graphing, they can also accommodate several lines of text and calculations at a time.

a. Bump mapping
c. Support vector machines

b. Genus
d. Graphing calculator

29. A _____ is a device for performing mathematical calculations, distinguished from a computer by having a limited problem solving ability and an interface optimized for interactive calculation rather than programming. _____s can be hardware or software, and mechanical or electronic, and are often built into devices such as PDAs or mobile phones.

Modern electronic _____s are generally small, digital, and usually inexpensive.

a. 1-center problem
c. Calculator

b. 2-3 heap
d. 120-cell

30. In mathematics, the _____ is a term used to describe the number of times one must apply a given operation to an integer before reaching a fixed point.

Usually, this refers to the additive or multiplicative persistence of an integer, which is how often one has to replace the number by the sum or product of its digits until one reaches a single digit. Because the numbers are broken down into their digits, the additive or multiplicative persistence depends on the radix.

a. Lychrel number
c. Coprime

b. Linear congruence theorem
d. Persistence of a number

31. In mathematics, the _____ or Pythagoras' theorem is a relation in Euclidean geometry among the three sides of a right triangle. The theorem is named after the Greek mathematician Pythagoras, who by tradition is credited with its discovery and proof, although it is often argued that knowledge of the theory predates him.. The theorem is as follows:

In any right triangle, the area of the square whose side is the hypotenuse is equal to the sum of the areas of the squares whose sides are the two legs.

Chapter 10. Trigonometry

a. 1-center problem
c. 2-3 heap
b. Pythagorean theorem
d. 120-cell

32. The _____ of a number are those digits that carry meaning contributing to its precision. This includes all digits except:

- leading and trailing zeros where they serve merely as placeholders to indicate the scale of the number.
- spurious digits introduced, for example, by calculations carried out to greater accuracy than that of the original data, or measurements reported to a greater precision than the equipment supports.

The concept of _____ is often used in connection with rounding. Rounding to n _____ is a more general-purpose technique than rounding to n decimal places, since it handles numbers of different scales in a uniform way. A practical calculation that uses any irrational number necessitates rounding the number, and hence the answer, to a finite number of _____.

a. Significant figures
c. Rounding
b. Shabakh
d. Tetration

33. In mathematics, a _____ is a statement that can be proved on the basis of explicitly stated or previously agreed assumptions.
   a. Boolean function
   c. Logical value
   b. Disjunction introduction
   d. Theorem

34. The Q-TIP of a geographic location is its height above a fixed reference point, often the mean sea level. _____, or geometric height, is mainly used when referring to points on the Earth's surface, while altitude or geopotential height is used for points above the surface, such as an aircraft in flight or a spacecraft in orbit.

Less commonly, _____ is measured using the center of the Earth as the reference point.

a. A posteriori
c. Elevation
b. A Mathematical Theory of Communication
d. A chemical equation

35. The _____ of an angle is the ratio of the length of the opposite side to the length of the hypotenuse. In our case

$$\sin A = \frac{\text{opposite}}{\text{hypotenuse}} = \frac{a}{h}.$$

Note that this ratio does not depend on size of the particular right triangle chosen, as long as it contains the angle A, since all such triangles are similar.

The cosine of an angle is the ratio of the length of the adjacent side to the length of the hypotenuse.

a. Law of sines
c. Right angle
b. Sine
d. Trigonometric functions

Chapter 10. Trigonometry

36. Johannes Müller von Königsberg, known by his Latin pseudonym _____, was an important German mathematician, astronomer and astrologer.

He was born in the Franconian village of Unfinden near Königsberg, Bavaria, not in the more famous Königsberg in East Prussia.

Thus, he is also called Johannes Müller, der Königsberger.

    a. Regiomontanus   b. Joseph Desch
    c. Riemann   d. Kenkichi Iwasawa

37. _____ is a quantity expressing the two-dimensional size of a defined part of a surface, typically a region bounded by a closed curve. The term surface _____ refers to the total _____ of the exposed surface of a 3-dimensional solid, such as the sum of the _____s of the exposed sides of a polyhedron. _____ is an important invariant in the differential geometry of surfaces.
    a. A chemical equation   b. A Mathematical Theory of Communication
    c. A posteriori   d. Area

38. In mathematics and in the sciences, a _____ (plural: _____e, formulæ or _____s) is a concise way of expressing information symbolically (as in a mathematical or chemical _____), or a general relationship between quantities. One of many famous _____e is Albert Einstein's E = mc^2 (see special relativity

In mathematics, a _____ is a key to solve an equation with variables. For example, the problem of determining the volume of a sphere is one that requires a significant amount of integral calculus to solve.

    a. 1-center problem   b. Formula
    c. 2-3 heap   d. 120-cell

39. In trigonometry and geometry, _____ is the process of determining the location of a point by measuring angles to it from known points at either end of a fixed baseline, rather than measuring distances to the point directly. The point can then be fixed as the third point of a triangle with one known side and two known angles.

_____ can also refer to the accurate surveying of systems of very large triangles, called _____ networks.

    a. 120-cell   b. 1-center problem
    c. 2-3 heap   d. Triangulation

40. In mathematics, a _____ is a function that repeats its values after some definite period has been added to its independent variable. This property is called periodicity. An illustration of a _____ with period P.

Everyday examples are seen when the variable is time; for instance the hands of a clock or the phases of the moon show periodic behaviour.

a. Calculus controversy
b. Method of indivisibles
c. Hyperbolic angle
d. Periodic function

41. In mathematics, a _____ is a circle with a unit radius. Frequently, especially in trigonometry, 'the' _____ is the circle of radius 1 centered at the origin in the Cartesian coordinate system in the Euclidean plane. The _____ is often denoted S^1; the generalization to higher dimensions is the unit sphere.
   a. Open unit disk
   b. Unit circle
   c. Inscribed angle theorem
   d. Excircle

42. A _____ is a simple shape of Euclidean geometry consisting of those points in a plane which are at a constant distance, called the radius, from a fixed point, called the center. A _____ with center A is sometimes denoted by the symbol A.

A chord of a _____ is a line segment whose two endpoints lie on the _____.

   a. Malfatti circles
   b. Circle
   c. Circular segment
   d. Circumcircle

43. In graph theory, a _____ in a graph is a sequence of vertices such that from each of its vertices there is an edge to the next vertex in the sequence. The first vertex is called the start vertex and the last vertex is called the end vertex. Both of them are called end or terminal vertices of the _____.
   a. Deltoid
   b. Path
   c. Blinding
   d. Class

44. In statistics, the _____ is the value that occurs the most frequently in a data set or a probability distribution. In some fields, notably education, sample data are often called scores, and the sample _____ is known as the modal score.

Like the statistical mean and the median, the _____ is a way of capturing important information about a random variable or a population in a single quantity.

   a. Function
   b. Field
   c. Deltoid
   d. Mode

45. The _____ is a unit of plane angle, equal to 180/π degrees, or about 57.2958 degrees. It is the standard unit of angular measurement in all areas of mathematics beyond the elementary level.

The _____ is represented by the symbol 'rad' or, more rarely, by the superscript c.

   a. 2-3 heap
   b. 120-cell
   c. Radian
   d. 1-center problem

Chapter 11. Counting Methods

1. In set theory, a _____ is a partially ordered set such that for each t ∈ T, the set {s ∈ T : s < t} is well-ordered by the relation <. For each t ∈ T, the order type of {s ∈ T : s < t} is called the height of t. The height of T itself is the least ordinal greater than the height of each element of T.
   - a. Set-theoretic topology
   - b. Definable numbers
   - c. Transitive reduction
   - d. Tree

2. A _____ is a 2D geometric symbolic representation of information according to some visualization technique. Sometimes, the technique uses a 3D visualization which is then projected onto the 2D surface. The word graph is sometimes used as a synonym for _____.
   - a. 2-3 heap
   - b. 120-cell
   - c. Diagram
   - d. 1-center problem

3. In category theory, an abstract branch of mathematics, an _____ of a category C is an object I in C such that for every object X in C, there exists precisely one morphism I → X. The dual notion is that of a terminal object: T is terminal if for every object X in C there exists a single morphism X → T. _____s are also called coterminal, and terminal objects are also called final.
   - a. A posteriori
   - b. A chemical equation
   - c. A Mathematical Theory of Communication
   - d. Initial object

4. In mathematics, hyperbolic n-space, denoted H^n, is the maximally symmetric, simply connected, n-dimensional Riemannian manifold with constant sectional curvature −1. _____ is the principal example of a space exhibiting hyperbolic geometry. It can be thought of as the negative-curvature analogue of the n-sphere.
   - a. Horocycle
   - b. Hyperbolic space
   - c. Margulis lemma
   - d. Hyperbolic geometry

5. In mathematics, the _____ of a non-negative integer n, denoted by n!, is the product of all positive integers less than or equal to n. For example,

$$5! = 1 \times 2 \times 3 \times 4 \times 5 = 120$$

and
$$6! = 1 \times 2 \times 3 \times 4 \times 5 \times 6 = 720$$

The notation n! was introduced by Christian Kramp in 1808.

The _____ function is formally defined by

$$n! = \prod_{k=1}^{n} k \qquad \forall n \in \mathbb{N}.$$

The above definition incorporates the instance

$$0! = 1$$

as an instance of the fact that the product of no numbers at all is 1.

   a. Plane partition
   b. Symbolic combinatorics
   c. Partition of a set
   d. Factorial

6. The _____ in operations research is a problem in discrete or combinatorial optimization. It is a prominent illustration of a class of problems in computational complexity theory which are classified as NP-hard.

The problem is: given a number of cities and the costs of travelling from any city to any other city, what is the least-cost round-trip route that visits each city exactly once and then returns to the starting city?

Given a number of cities and the costs of travelling from any city to any other city, what is the least-cost round-trip route that visits each city exactly once and then returns to the starting city?

The size of the solution space is!/2 for n > 2, where n is the number of cities.

   a. Travelling salesman problem
   b. Snake-in-the-box
   c. Cut vertex
   d. New digraph reconstruction conjecture

7. In combinatorial mathematics, a _____ is an un-ordered collection of distinct elements, usually of a prescribed size and taken from a given set. Given such a set S, a _____ of elements of S is just a subset of S, where as always forsets the order of the elements is not taken into account. Also, as always forsets, no elements can be repeated more than once in a _____; this is often referred to as a 'collection without repetition'.

   a. Fill-in
   b. Heawood number
   c. Sparsity
   d. Combination

8. In mathematics and in the sciences, a _____ (plural: _____e, formulæ or _____s) is a concise way of expressing information symbolically (as in a mathematical or chemical _____), or a general relationship between quantities. One of many famous _____e is Albert Einstein's E = mc^2 (see special relativity

In mathematics, a _____ is a key to solve an equation with variables. For example, the problem of determining the volume of a sphere is one that requires a significant amount of integral calculus to solve.

   a. 2-3 heap
   b. 120-cell
   c. 1-center problem
   d. Formula

9. In several fields of mathematics the term _____ is used with different but closely related meanings. They all relate to the notion of mapping the elements of a set to other elements of the same set, i.e., exchanging elements of a set.

The general concept of _____ can be defined more formally in different contexts:

In combinatorics, a _____ is usually understood to be a sequence containing each element from a finite set once, and only once.

a. Tensor product
b. Cyclic permutation
c. Linearly independent
d. Permutation

10. In cryptography, a _____ is an algorithm for performing encryption and decryption -- a series of well-defined steps that can be followed as a procedure. An alternative term is encipherment. In non-technical usage, a '_____' is the same thing as a 'code'; however, the concepts are distinct in cryptography.

a. Group key
b. Polygraphic substitution
c. Transmission security
d. Cipher

11. In _____, the probability of many events can be determined by direct calculation In most cases, the probabilities and odds are approximations due to rounding.

a. 2-3 heap
b. Poker
c. 1-center problem
d. 120-cell

12. A _____ is one of the basic shapes of geometry: a polygon with three corners or vertices and three sides or edges which are line segments. A _____ with vertices A, B, and C is denoted ABC.

In Euclidean geometry any three non-collinear points determine a unique _____ and a unique plane.

a. Kepler triangle
b. 1-center problem
c. Fuhrmann circle
d. Triangle

13. In elementary algebra, a _____ is a polynomial with two terms: the sum of two monomials. It is the simplest kind of polynomial except for a monomial.

The _____ $a^2 - b^2$ can be factored as the product of two other _____s:

$a^2 - b^2$.

The product of a pair of linear _____s a x + b and c x + d is:

2 +x + bd.

A _____ raised to the nth power, represented as

n

can be expanded by means of the _____ theorem or, equivalently, using Pascal's triangle.

a. Rational root theorem
b. Binomial
c. Real structure
d. Cylindrical algebraic decomposition

14. In mathematics, the _____ $\binom{n}{k}$ is the coefficient of the x^k term in the polynomial expansion of the binomial power ^{n}.

In combinatorics, $\binom{n}{k}$ is interpreted as the number of k-element subsets of an n-element set, that is the number of ways that k things can be 'chosen' from a set of n things. Hence, $\binom{n}{k}$ is often read as 'n choose k' and called the choose function of n and k.

    a. Rule of product
    b. Symbolic combinatorics
    c. Dyson conjecture
    d. Binomial coefficient

15. In mathematics, the _____ is an important formula giving the expansion of powers of sums. Its simplest version states that

$$(x+y)^n = \sum_{k=0}^{n} \binom{n}{k} x^{n-k} y^k \qquad (1)$$

for any real or complex numbers x and y, and any nonnegative integer n. The binomial coefficient appearing in may be defined in terms of the factorial function n!:

$$\binom{n}{k} = \frac{n!}{k!\,(n-k)!}.$$

For example, here are the cases where 2 ≤ n ≤ 5:

$$(x+y)^2 = x^2 + 2xy + y^2$$
$$(x+y)^3 = x^3 + 3x^2y + 3xy^2 + y^3$$
$$(x+y)^4 = x^4 + 4x^3y + 6x^2y^2 + 4xy^3 + y^4$$
$$(x+y)^5 = x^5 + 5x^4y + 10x^3y^2 + 10x^2y^3 + 5xy^4 + y^5.$$

Formula is valid more generally for any elements x and y of a semiring as long as xy = yx..

    a. Stirling transform
    b. Hypergeometric identities
    c. Lah numbers
    d. Binomial theorem

16. In mathematics, a _____ is a constant multiplicative factor of a certain object. For example, in the expression $9x^2$, the _____ of x^2 is 9.

The object can be such things as a variable, a vector, a function, etc.

    a. Multivariate division algorithm
    b. Fibonacci polynomials
    c. Stability radius
    d. Coefficient

17. In mathematics, a _____ is a statement that can be proved on the basis of explicitly stated or previously agreed assumptions.
   a. Logical value
   b. Disjunction introduction
   c. Theorem
   d. Boolean function

128   *Chapter 12. Probability*

1. _____ is the likelihood or chance that something is the case or will happen. Theoretical _____ is used extensively in areas such as statistics, mathematics, science and philosophy to draw conclusions about the likelihood of potential events and the underlying mechanics of complex systems.

The word _____ does not have a consistent direct definition.

  a. Standardized moment   b. Statistical significance
  c. Discrete random variable   d. Probability

2. In elementary algebra, a _____ is a polynomial with two terms: the sum of two monomials. It is the simplest kind of polynomial except for a monomial.

The _____ $a^2 - b^2$ can be factored as the product of two other _____s:

$a^2 - b^2$.

The product of a pair of linear _____s a x + b and c x + d is:

2 +x + bd.

A _____ raised to the nth power, represented as

n

can be expanded by means of the _____ theorem or, equivalently, using Pascal's triangle.

  a. Real structure   b. Binomial
  c. Cylindrical algebraic decomposition   d. Rational root theorem

3. _____ (May 16 [O.S. May 4] 1821 - December 8 [O.S. November 26] 1894) was a Russian mathematician. His name can be alternatively transliterated as Chebychev, Chebyshov, Tchebycheff or Tschebyscheff .

One of nine children, Chebyshev was born in the village of Okatovo in the district of Borovsk, province of Kaluga.

  a. Fibonacci   b. Serre
  c. Pafnuty Lvovich Chebyshev   d. Girard Desargues

4. _____ is the philosophical proposition that every event, including human cognition and behavior, decision and action, is causally determined by an unbroken chain of prior occurrences. With numerous historical debates, many varieties and philosophical positions on the subject of _____ exist from traditions throughout the world.

It is a popular misconception that _____ necessarily entails that humanity or individual humans have no influence on the future and its events; however, determinists believe that the level to which human beings have influence over their future is itself dependent on present and past.

Chapter 12. Probability

a. Philosophy of mathematics
b. Philosophy
c. Mutually exclusive
d. Determinism

5. In probability theory, an _____ is a set of outcomes to which a probability is assigned. Typically, when the sample space is finite, any subset of the sample space is an _____. However, this approach does not work well in cases where the sample space is infinite, most notably when the outcome is a real number.
   a. Audio compression
   b. Information set
   c. Equaliser
   d. Event

6. In scientific inquiry, an _____ is a method of investigating particular types of research questions or solving particular types of problems. The _____ is a cornerstone in the empirical approach to acquiring deeper knowledge about the world and is used in both natural sciences as well as in social sciences. An _____ is defined, in science, as a method of investigating less known fields, solving practical problems and proving theoretical assumptions.
   a. Experiment
   b. A posteriori
   c. A Mathematical Theory of Communication
   d. A chemical equation

7. _____ IPA: [pjɛʁ ɛ dɵfɛʁ 'ma] (17 August 1601 or 1607/8 - 12 January 1665) was a French lawyer at the Parlement of Toulouse, France, and a mathematician who is given credit for early developments that led to modern calculus. In particular, he is recognized for his discovery of an original method of finding the greatest and the smallest ordinates of curved lines, which is analogous to that of the then unknown differential calculus, as well as his research into the theory of numbers. He also made notable contributions to analytic geometry, probability, and optics.
   a. Nikita Borisov
   b. Philip J. Davis
   c. Felix Hausdorff
   d. Pierre de Fermat

8. In game theory, an _____ is a set of moves or strategies taken by the players, or their payoffs resulting from the actions or strategies taken by all players. The two are complementary in that given knowledge of the set of strategies of all players, the final state of the game is known, as are any relevant payoffs. In a game where chance or a random event is involved, the _____ is not known from only the set of strategies, but is only realized when the random even are realized.
   a. Autonomous system
   b. Algebraic
   c. Equaliser
   d. Outcome

9. The word _____ denotes information gained by means of observation, experience as opposed to theoretical. A central concept in science and the scientific method is that all evidence must be _____ that is, dependent on evidence or consequences that are observable by the senses. It is usually differentiated from the philosophic usage of empiricism by the use of the adjective '_____' or the adverb 'empirically.' '_____' as an adjective or adverb is used in conjunction with both the natural and social sciences, and refers to the use of working hypotheses that are testable using observation or experiment.
   a. A Mathematical Theory of Communication
   b. A posteriori
   c. A chemical equation
   d. Empirical

10. _____ or experimental probability, is the ratio of the number favorable outcomes to the total number of trials , not in a sample space but in an actual sequence of experiments. In a more general sense, _____ estimates probabilities from experience and observation. The phrase a posteriori probability has also been used an alternative to _____ or relative frequency.

a. A chemical equation
b. A Mathematical Theory of Communication
c. A posteriori
d. Empirical probability

11. _____ (April 14, 1629 - July 8, 1695) was a prominent Dutch mathematician, astronomer, physicist, and horologist. His work included early telescopic studies, investigations and inventions related to time keeping, and studies of both optics and centrifugal force.

_____ was born in The Hague, the son of Constantijn Huygens, a friend of René Descartes.

a. Abraham Sinkov
b. Christiaan Huygens
c. Agnes Meyer Driscoll
d. Adi Shamir

12. The _____ is identified with the works of Pierre Simon Laplace. As stated in his Théorie analytique des probabilités,

> The probability of an event is the ratio of the number of cases favorable to it, to the number of all cases possible when nothing leads us to expect that any one of these cases should occur more than any other, which renders them, for us, equally possible.

This definition is essentially a consequence of the principle of indifference.

a. Classical definition of Probability
b. 120-cell
c. Frequency probability
d. 1-center problem

13. In mathematics and physics, there are a _____ number of topics named in honor of Leonhard Euler . As well, many of these topics include their own unique function, equation, formula, identity, number, or other mathematical entity. Unfortunately however, many of these entities have been given simple names like Euler's function, Euler's equation, and Euler's formula, which are further confused by variations of the 'Euler'-prefix Overall though, Euler's work touched upon so many fields that he is often the earliest written reference on a given matter.

a. List of trigonometry topics
b. List of integrals of logarithmic functions
c. Large
d. List of mathematical knots and links

14. The _____ is a theorem in probability that describes the long-term stability of the mean of a random variable. Given a random variable with a finite expected value, if its values are repeatedly sampled, as the number of these observations increases, their mean will tend to approach and stay close to the expected value.

The LLN can easily be illustrated using the rolls of a die.

a. Graphical model
b. Point process
c. Random field
d. Law of large numbers

15. _____ , a discipline of biology, is the science of heredity and variation in living organisms. The fact that living things inherit traits from their parents has been used since prehistoric times to improve crop plants and animals through selective breeding. However, the modern science of _____, which seeks to understand the process of inheritance, only began with the work of Gregor Mendel in the mid-nineteenth century.

Chapter 12. Probability

a. Genetics
b. Fitness landscapes
c. Polytomy
d. Hardy-Weinberg principle

16. In probability theory and statistics the _____ in favour of an event or a proposition are the quantity p /, where p is the probability of the event or proposition. The _____ against the same event are / p. For example, if you chose a random day of the week, then the _____ that you would choose a Sunday would be 1/6, not 1/7.
   a. Odds
   b. Anscombe transform
   c. Estimation of covariance matrices
   d. Event

17. In discrete mathematics and predominantly in set theory, a _____ is a concept used in comparisons of sets to refer to the unique values of one set in relation to another. The terms 'absolute' and 'relative' _____ refer to more specific applications of the concept, with universal _____s referring to elements unique to the universal set and the latter referring to the unique elements of one set in relation to another. In this image, the universal set is represented by the border of the image, and the set A as a disc.
   a. Complement
   b. Derivative algebra
   c. Kernel
   d. Huge

18. In simple terms, two events are _____ if they cannot occur at the same time.

In logic, two _____ propositions are propositions that logically cannot both be true. To say that more than two propositions are _____ may, depending on context mean that no two of them can both be true, or only that they cannot all be true.

   a. Philosophy of mathematics
   b. Philosophy
   c. Determinism
   d. Mutually exclusive

19. In differential geometry, a discipline within mathematics, a _____ is a subset of the tangent bundle of a manifold satisfying certain properties. _____s are used to build up notions of integrability, and specifically of a foliation of a manifold
   a. Discontinuity
   b. Coherence
   c. Constraint
   d. Distribution

20. In probability theory and statistics, a _____ identifies either the probability of each value of an unidentified random variable, or the probability of the value falling within a particular interval. The probability function describes the range of possible values that a random variable can attain and the probability that the value of the random variable is within any subset of that range.

When the random variable takes values in the set of real numbers, the _____ is completely described by the cumulative distribution function, whose value at each real x is the probability that the random variable is smaller than or equal to x.

   a. Statistical graphics
   b. Probability distribution
   c. Normal distribution
   d. Z-test

Chapter 12. Probability

21. In mathematics, _____ are used in the study of chance and probability. They were developed to assist in the analysis of games of chance, stochastic events, and the results of scientific experiments by capturing only the mathematical properties necessary to answer probabilistic questions. Further formalizations have firmly grounded the entity in the theoretical domains of mathematics by making use of measure theory.
    a. Statistics
    b. Median polish
    c. Random variables
    d. Statistical dispersion

22. In probability theory, a probability distribution is called _____ if its cumulative distribution function is _____. That is equivalent to saying that for random variables X with the distribution in question, Pr[X = a] = 0 for all real numbers a. If the distribution of X is _____ then X is called a _____ random variable.
    a. Continuous
    b. Conull set
    c. Concatenated codes
    d. Continuous phase modulation

23. A _____ is the transfer of an interest in property (or in law the equivalent - a charge) to a lender as a security for a debt - usually a loan of money. While a _____ in itself is not a debt, it is lender's security for a debt. It is a transfer of an interest in land (or the equivalent), from the owner to the _____ lender, on the condition that this interest will be returned to the owner of the real estate when the terms of the _____ have been satisfied or performed.
    a. 1-center problem
    b. 120-cell
    c. 2-3 heap
    d. Mortgage

24. In statistics, an _____ comes from two variables that are related and is often confused with causality though _____ does not imply a causal relationship. In formal statistics, correlation and _____ are related but not entirely overlapping concepts.

For example, the United Nations studied governmental failure--when governments fall or are overthrown and found that the best indicator of a government about to fall was the infant mortality rate.

    a. Outcome
    b. Association
    c. Integration
    d. Efficiency

25. _____ is the probability of some event A, given the occurrence of some other event B. _____ is written P[A | B], and is read 'the probability of A, given B'.

Joint probability is the probability of two events in conjunction. That is, it is the probability of both events together. The joint probability of A and B is written $P(A \cap B)$ or $P(A,B)$.

    a. Sample space
    b. Conditional Probability
    c. Quantile
    d. Renewal theory

26. _____ is the mathematical operation of scaling one number by another. It is one of the four basic operations in elementary arithmetic.

_____ is defined for whole numbers in terms of repeated addition; for example, 4 multiplied by 3 can be calculated by adding 3 copies of 4 together:

$$4 + 4 + 4 = 12.$$

_____ of rational numbers and real numbers is defined by systematic generalization of this basic idea.

- a. The number 0 is even.
- b. Highest common factor
- c. Least common multiple
- d. Multiplication

27. Introduction

In the theory of probability and statistics, a _____ is an experiment whose outcome is random and can be either of two possible outcomes, 'success' and 'failure'.

In practice it refers to a single experiment which can have one of two possible outcomes. These events can be phrased into 'yes or no' questions:

- Did the coin land heads?
- Was the newborn child a girl?
- Were a person's eyes green?
- Did a mosquito die after the area was sprayed with insecticide?
- Did a potential customer decide to buy a product?
- Did a citizen vote for a specific candidate?
- Did an employee vote pro-union?

Therefore success and failure are labels for outcomes, and should not be construed literally. Examples of _____s include

- Flipping a coin. In this context, obverse conventionally denotes success and reverse denotes failure. A fair coin has the probability of success 0.5 by definition.
- Rolling a die, where a six is 'success' and everything else a 'failure'.
- In conducting a political opinion poll, choosing a voter at random to ascertain whether that voter will vote 'yes' in an upcoming referendum.

Mathematically, a _____ can be described by a sample space Ω consisting of two values, s for 'success' and f for 'failure'. Therefore the sample space is $\Omega = \{s, f\}$.

- a. Bernoulli trial
- b. Marginal distribution
- c. Law of total cumulance
- d. Point process

28. _____ typically deals with the probability of several successive decisions, each of which has two possible outcomes.

The probability of an event can be expressed as a _____ if its outcomes can be broken down into two probabilities p and q, where p and q are complementary For example, tossing a coin can be either heads or tails, each which have a probability of 0.5. Rolling a four on a six-sided die can be expressed as the probability of getting a 4 or the probability of rolling something else.

    a. Markov chain
    c. Quantile
    b. Marginal distribution
    d. Binomial probability

29. In mathematics, hyperbolic n-space, denoted H^n, is the maximally symmetric, simply connected, n-dimensional Riemannian manifold with constant sectional curvature −1. _____ is the principal example of a space exhibiting hyperbolic geometry. It can be thought of as the negative-curvature analogue of the n-sphere.

    a. Hyperbolic geometry
    c. Margulis lemma
    b. Horocycle
    d. Hyperbolic space

30. In mathematics and in the sciences, a _____ (plural: _____e, formulæ or _____s) is a concise way of expressing information symbolically (as in a mathematical or chemical _____), or a general relationship between quantities. One of many famous _____e is Albert Einstein's E = mc^2 (see special relativity

In mathematics, a _____ is a key to solve an equation with variables. For example, the problem of determining the volume of a sphere is one that requires a significant amount of integral calculus to solve.

    a. Formula
    c. 2-3 heap
    b. 120-cell
    d. 1-center problem

31. In probability theory and statistics, the _____ of a random variable is the integral of the random variable with respect to its probability measure. For discrete random variables this is equivalent to the probability-weighted sum of the possible values, and for continuous random variables with a density function it is the probability density -weighted integral of the possible values.

The _____ may be intuitively understood by the law of large numbers: The _____, when it exists, is almost surely the limit of the sample mean as sample size grows to infinity.

    a. Infinitely divisible distribution
    c. Expected value
    b. Event
    d. Illustration

32. A _____ is a structured activity, usually undertaken for enjoyment and sometimes also used as an educational tool. _____s are distinct from work, which is usually carried out for remuneration, and from art, which is more concerned with the expression of ideas. However, the distinction is not clear-cut, and many _____s are also considered to be work (such as professional players of spectator sports/_____s) or art (such as jigsaw puzzles or _____s involving an artistic layout such as Mah-jongg solitaire.)

    a. 120-cell
    c. 2-3 heap
    b. 1-center problem
    d. Game

Chapter 12. Probability

33. _____ is a casino and gambling game named after the French word meaning 'small wheel'. In the game, players may choose to place bets on either a number, a range of numbers, the color red or black, or whether the number is odd or even. To determine the winning number and color, a croupier spins a wheel in one direction, then spins a ball in the opposite direction around a tilted circular track running around the circumference of the wheel.

   a. 2-3 heap
   b. 120-cell
   c. 1-center problem
   d. Roulette

34. _____ is a widely used class of computational algorithms for simulating the behavior of various physical and mathematical systems, and for other computations.

   a. 1-center problem
   b. 2-3 heap
   c. Monte Carlo method
   d. 120-cell

35. _____ are a class of computational algorithms that rely on repeated random sampling to compute their results. _____ are often used when simulating physical and mathematical systems. Because of their reliance on repeated computation and random or pseudo-random numbers, _____ are most suited to calculation by a computer.

   a. Normal distribution
   b. Monte Carlo methods
   c. Regression toward the mean
   d. Biplot

36. In mathematics, the _____ is a term used to describe the number of times one must apply a given operation to an integer before reaching a fixed point.

Usually, this refers to the additive or multiplicative persistence of an integer, which is how often one has to replace the number by the sum or product of its digits until one reaches a single digit. Because the numbers are broken down into their digits, the additive or multiplicative persistence depends on the radix.

   a. Linear congruence theorem
   b. Coprime
   c. Lychrel number
   d. Persistence of a number

37. Let $U = \{U_n\}_{n \in \mathbb{N}}$ be a uniform ensemble and $X = \{X_n\}_{n \in \mathbb{N}}$ be an ensemble. The ensemble X is called _____ if X and U are indistinguishable in polynomial time.

   a. 120-cell
   b. Pseudorandom number sequence
   c. 1-center problem
   d. Pseudorandom

Chapter 13. Statistics

1. The _____ fallacy is an informal fallacy. It ascribes cause where none exists. The flaw is failing to account for natural fluctuations.
   a. Degrees of freedom
   b. Differential
   c. Regression
   d. Depth

2. _____ is a process of gathering, modeling, and transforming data with the goal of highlighting useful information, suggesting conclusions, and supporting decision making. _____ has multiple facets and approaches, encompassing diverse techniques under a variety of names, in different business, science, and social science domains.

   Data mining is a particular _____ technique that focuses on modeling and knowledge discovery for predictive rather than purely descriptive purposes.

   a. Power transform
   b. Data analysis
   c. Subgroup analysis
   d. Double mass analysis

3. _____ are used to describe the basic features of the data gathered from an experimental study in various ways. A _____ is distinguished from inductive statistics. They provide simple summaries about the sample and the measures.
   a. Null hypothesis
   b. Biostatistics
   c. Failure rate
   d. Descriptive statistics

4. _____ is an approach to analyzing data for the purpose of formulating hypotheses worth testing, complementing the tools of conventional statistics for testing hypotheses. It was so named by John Tukey.

   Tukey held that too much emphasis in statistics was placed on statistical hypothesis testing; more emphasis needed to be placed on using data to suggest hypotheses to test.

   a. Exploratory data analysis
   b. Explained variation
   c. Overdispersion
   d. Index of dispersion

5. Induction or _____, sometimes called inductive logic, is the process of reasoning in which the premises of an argument are believed to support the conclusion but do not entail it;. Induction is a form of reasoning that makes generalizations based on individual instances. It is used to ascribe properties or relations to types based on an observation instance; or to formulate laws based on limited observations of recurring phenomenal patterns.
   a. Idempotency of entailment
   b. Affine logic
   c. Intuitionistic logic
   d. Inductive reasoning

6. The _____ of a material is defined as its mass per unit volume:

$$\rho = \frac{m}{V}$$

Different materials usually have different densities, so _____ is an important concept regarding buoyancy, metal purity and packaging.

In some cases _____ is expressed as the dimensionless quantities specific gravity or relative _____, in which case it is expressed in multiples of the _____ of some other standard material, usually water or air.

In a well-known story, Archimedes was given the task of determining whether King Hiero's goldsmith was embezzling gold during the manufacture of a wreath dedicated to the gods and replacing it with another, cheaper alloy.

a. 120-cell
b. 1-center problem
c. Density
d. 2-3 heap

7. In mathematics, hyperbolic n-space, denoted H^n, is the maximally symmetric, simply connected, n-dimensional Riemannian manifold with constant sectional curvature −1. _____ is the principal example of a space exhibiting hyperbolic geometry. It can be thought of as the negative-curvature analogue of the n-sphere.
a. Hyperbolic geometry
b. Hyperbolic space
c. Horocycle
d. Margulis lemma

8. In graph theory, a _____ in a graph is a sequence of vertices such that from each of its vertices there is an edge to the next vertex in the sequence. The first vertex is called the start vertex and the last vertex is called the end vertex. Both of them are called end or terminal vertices of the _____.
a. Blinding
b. Path
c. Class
d. Deltoid

9. A _____ is the result of applying a function to a set of data.

More formally, statistical theory defines a _____ as a function of a sample where the function itself is independent of the sample's distribution: the term is used both for the function and for the value of the function on a given sample.

A _____ is distinct from an unknown statistical parameter, which is not computable from a sample.

a. Spatial dependence
b. Loss function
c. Parameter space
d. Statistic

10. _____ is a mathematical science pertaining to the collection, analysis, interpretation or explanation, and presentation of data. It also provides tools for prediction and forecasting based on data. It is applicable to a wide variety of academic disciplines, from the natural and social sciences to the humanities, government and business.
a. Statistics
b. Regression toward the mean
c. Probability distribution
d. Percentile rank

11. In statistics the _____ of an event i is the number n_i of times the event occurred in the experiment or the study. These frequencies are often graphically represented in histograms.

We speak of absolute frequencies, when the counts n_i themselves are given and of

$$f_i = \frac{n_i}{N} = \frac{n_i}{\sum_i n_i}$$

Chapter 13. Statistics

Taking the f_i for all i and tabulating or plotting them leads to a _____ distribution.

- a. Frequency
- b. Digital room correction
- c. Robinson-Dadson curves
- d. Subharmonic

12. In statistics, a _____ is a list of the values that a variable takes in a sample. It is usually a list, ordered by quantity, showing the number of times each value appears. For example, if 100 people rate a five-point Likert scale assessing their agreement with a statement on a scale on which 1 denotes strong agreement and 5 strong disagreement, the _____ of their responses might look like:

This simple tabulation has two drawbacks.

- a. Covariance
- b. Frequency distribution
- c. Confounding
- d. Percentile

13. A _____ typically refers to a class of handheld calculators that are capable of plotting graphs, solving simultaneous equations, and performing numerous other tasks with variables. Most popular _____s are also programmable, allowing the user to create customized programs, typically for scientific/engineering and education applications. Due to their large displays intended for graphing, they can also accommodate several lines of text and calculations at a time.
- a. Genus
- b. Bump mapping
- c. Support vector machines
- d. Graphing calculator

14. The term qualitative is used to describe certain types of information. _____ are described in terms of quality. This is the converse of quantitative, which more precisely describes data in terms of quantity and often using a numerical figure to represent something in a statement.
- a. Level of measurement
- b. Nominal category
- c. Qualitative data
- d. Missing values

15. A _____ is a device for performing mathematical calculations, distinguished from a computer by having a limited problem solving ability and an interface optimized for interactive calculation rather than programming. _____s can be hardware or software, and mechanical or electronic, and are often built into devices such as PDAs or mobile phones.

Modern electronic _____s are generally small, digital, and usually inexpensive.

- a. Calculator
- b. 1-center problem
- c. 2-3 heap
- d. 120-cell

16. In differential geometry, a discipline within mathematics, a _____ is a subset of the tangent bundle of a manifold satisfying certain properties. _____s are used to build up notions of integrability, and specifically of a foliation of a manifold
- a. Constraint
- b. Distribution
- c. Discontinuity
- d. Coherence

17. The _____ or Dirac's delta is a mathematical construct introduced by the British theoretical physicist Paul Dirac. Informally, it is a function representing an infinitely sharp peak bounding unit area: a function that has the value zero everywhere except at x = 0 where its value is infinitely large in such a way that its total integral is 1. It is a continuous analogue of the discrete Kronecker delta.
 a. Hyperfunction   b. Schwartz kernel theorem
 c. Weak derivative   d. Dirac delta

18. The mathematical concept of a _____ expresses the intuitive idea of deterministic dependence between two quantities, one of which is viewed as primary and the other as secondary. A _____ then is a way to associate a unique output for each input of a specified type, for example, a real number or an element of a given set.
 a. Coherent   b. Going up
 c. Grill   d. Function

19. In mathematics, the _____ functions are functions of an angle; they are important when studying triangles and modeling periodic phenomena, among many other applications.
 a. Law of sines   b. Coversine
 c. Gudermannian function   d. Trigonometric

20. In mathematics, the _____ are functions of an angle. They are important in the study of triangles and modeling periodic phenomena, among many other applications. _____ are commonly defined as ratios of two sides of a right triangle containing the angle, and can equivalently be defined as the lengths of various line segments from a unit circle.
 a. Sine   b. Law of sines
 c. Trigonometric integrals   d. Trigonometric functions

21. In statistics, a _____ is a graphical display of tabulated frequencies, shown as bars. It shows what proportion of cases fall into each of several categories. A _____ differs from a bar chart in that it is the area of the bar that denotes the value, not the height as in bar charts, a crucial distinction when the categories are not of uniform width.
 a. Histogram   b. First-hitting-time models
 c. Probability distribution   d. Standardized moment

22. In geometry a _____ is traditionally a plane figure that is bounded by a closed path or circuit, composed of a finite sequence of straight line segments. These segments are called its edges or sides, and the points where two edges meet are the _____'s vertices or corners. The interior of the _____ is sometimes called its body.
 a. Regular polygon   b. Polygon
 c. Polygonal curve   d. Parallelogon

23. _____ are used in computer graphics to compose images that are three-dimensional in appearance. Usually triangular, _____ arise when an object's surface is modeled, vertices are selected, and the object is rendered in a wire frame model. This is quicker to display than a shaded model; thus the _____ are a stage in computer animation.
 a. Triskaidecagon   b. Heptadecagon
 c. Polygons   d. Visibility polygon

24. In set theory and its applications throughout mathematics, a _____ is a collection of sets that can be unambiguously defined by a property that all its members share. The precise definition of '_____' depends on foundational context. In work on ZF set theory, the notion of _____ is informal, whereas other set theories, such as NBG set theory, axiomatize the notion of '_____'.

a. Congruent
b. Filter
c. Coherence
d. Class

25. In mathematics, the concept of a '_____' is used to describe the behavior of a function as its argument or input either 'gets close' to some point, or as the argument becomes arbitrarily large; or the behavior of a sequence's elements as their index increases indefinitely. _____s are used in calculus and other branches of mathematical analysis to define derivatives and continuity.

In formulas, _____ is usually abbreviated as lim.

a. Contact
b. Limit
c. Duality
d. Copula

26. In mathematics, a _____ of a set S in a topological space X is a point x in X that can be 'approximated' by points of S other than x itself. This concept profitably generalizes the notion of a limit and is the underpinning of concepts such as closed set and topological closure. Indeed, a set is closed if and only if it contains all of its _____s, and the topological closure operation can be thought of as an operation that enriches a set by adding its _____s.

a. 2-3 heap
b. 120-cell
c. Limit point
d. 1-center problem

27. The word _____ denotes information gained by means of observation, experience as opposed to theoretical. A central concept in science and the scientific method is that all evidence must be _____ that is, dependent on evidence or consequences that are observable by the senses. It is usually differentiated from the philosophic usage of empiricism by the use of the adjective '_____' or the adverb 'empirically.' '_____' as an adjective or adverb is used in conjunction with both the natural and social sciences, and refers to the use of working hypotheses that are testable using observation or experiment.

a. A Mathematical Theory of Communication
b. Empirical
c. A posteriori
d. A chemical equation

28. A bar chart or _____ is a chart with rectangular bars with lengths proportional to the values that they represent. Bar charts are used for comparing two or more values. The bars can be horizontally or vertically oriented.

a. Bar graph
b. 2-3 heap
c. 1-center problem
d. 120-cell

29. A _____ is a circular chart divided into sectors, illustrating relative magnitudes or frequences or percents. In a _____, the arc length of each sector, is proportional to the quantity it represents. Together, the sectors create a full disk.

a. 2-3 heap
b. 1-center problem
c. 120-cell
d. Pie chart

30. _____ or experimental probability, is the ratio of the number favorable outcomes to the total number of trials , not in a sample space but in an actual sequence of experiments. In a more general sense, _____ estimates probabilities from experience and observation. The phrase a posteriori probability has also been used an alternative to _____ or relative frequency.

a. A Mathematical Theory of Communication
b. Empirical probability
c. A posteriori
d. A chemical equation

Chapter 13. Statistics

31. _____ is the likelihood or chance that something is the case or will happen. Theoretical _____ is used extensively in areas such as statistics, mathematics, science and philosophy to draw conclusions about the likelihood of potential events and the underlying mechanics of complex systems.

The word _____ does not have a consistent direct definition.

  a. Standardized moment
  c. Discrete random variable
  b. Probability
  d. Statistical significance

32. In elementary algebra, a _____ is a polynomial with two terms: the sum of two monomials. It is the simplest kind of polynomial except for a monomial.

The _____ $a^2 - b^2$ can be factored as the product of two other _____ s:

  $a^2 - b^2$.

The product of a pair of linear _____ s a x + b and c x + d is:

  2 +x + bd.

A _____ raised to the nth power, represented as

  n

can be expanded by means of the _____ theorem or, equivalently, using Pascal's triangle.

  a. Cylindrical algebraic decomposition
  c. Real structure
  b. Binomial
  d. Rational root theorem

33. In mathematics, an average, or _____ of a data set refers to a measure of the 'middle' or 'expected' value of the data set. There are many different descriptive statistics that can be chosen as a measurement of the _____ of the data items.

An average is a single value that is meant to typify a list of values.

  a. Trimean
  c. Quartile
  b. Central tendency
  d. Mean reciprocal rank

34. In statistics, _____ has two related meanings:

- the arithmetic _____.
- the expected value of a random variable, which is also called the population _____.

It is sometimes stated that the '_____' _____s average. This is incorrect if '_____' is taken in the specific sense of 'arithmetic _____' as there are different types of averages: the _____, median, and mode. For instance, average house prices almost always use the median value for the average.

For a real-valued random variable X, the _____ is the expectation of X.

   a. Statistical population   b. Probability
   c. Proportional hazards model   d. Mean

35. In descriptive statistics, a _____ is a convenient way of graphically depicting the five-number summary, which consists of the smallest observation, lower quartile (Q1), median, upper quartile (Q3), and largest observation; in addition, the _____ indicates which observations, if any, are considered unusual, or outliers.
   a. Box plot   b. Non-linear least squares
   c. Mathematical model   d. Point-slope form

36. In mathematics the concept of a _____ generalizes notions such as 'length', 'area', and 'volume'. Informally, given some base set, a '_____' is any consistent assignment of 'sizes' to the subsets of the base set. Depending on the application, the 'size' of a subset may be interpreted as its physical size, the amount of something that lies within the subset, or the probability that some random process will yield a result within the subset.
   a. Measure   b. Lattice
   c. Cusp   d. Congruent

37. A _____ is is a graphical technique for presenting a data set drawn by hand or produced by a mechanical or electronic plotter. It is a graph depicting the relationship between two or more variables used, for instance, in visualising scientific data.

_____s play an important role in statistics and data analysis.

   a. C-35   b. Lattice
   c. Dini   d. Plot

38. The _____ is similar to an arithmetic mean, where instead of each of the data points contributing equally to the final average, some data points contribute more than others. The notion of _____ plays a role in descriptive statistics and also occurs in a more general form in several other areas of mathematics.

If all the weights are equal, then the _____ is the same as the arithmetic mean.

   a. Truncated mean   b. Mid-range
   c. Quasi-arithmetic mean   d. Weighted mean

39. In statistics, an _____ is an observation that is numerically distant from the rest of the data. Statistics derived from data sets that include _____s may be misleading. For example, if one is calculating the average temperature of 10 objects in a room, and most are between 20 and 25 degrees Celsius, but an oven is at 175 °C, the median of the data may be 23 °C but the mean temperature will be between 35.5 and 40 °C.

a. Outlier
b. A Mathematical Theory of Communication
c. A posteriori
d. A chemical equation

40. In geometry, a _____ of a triangle is a line segment joining a vertex to the midpoint of the opposing side. Every triangle has exactly three _____s; one running from each vertex to the opposite side.

The three _____s are concurrent at a point known as the triangle's centroid, or center of mass of the triangle.

a. Statistical significance
b. Median
c. Percentile rank
d. Correlation

41. In statistics, the _____ is the value that occurs the most frequently in a data set or a probability distribution. In some fields, notably education, sample data are often called scores, and the sample _____ is known as the modal score.

Like the statistical mean and the median, the _____ is a way of capturing important information about a random variable or a population in a single quantity.

a. Mode
b. Deltoid
c. Field
d. Function

42. In statistics, a _____ is a continuous probability distribution with two different modes. These appear as distinct peaks in the probability density function, as shown in Figure 1.

Examples of variables with _____s include the time between eruptions of certain geysers, the color of galaxies, the size of worker weaver ants, the age of incidence of Hodgkin's lymphoma, the speed of inactivation of the drug isoniazid in US adults, and the absolute magnitude of novae.

a. Fat tail
b. Singular distribution
c. Bimodal distribution
d. Phase-type distribution

43. A _____ is a collection of data, usually presented in tabular form. Each column represents a particular variable. Each row corresponds to a given member of the _____ in question.
a. 1-center problem
b. 120-cell
c. Data set
d. 2-3 heap

44. _____ generally conveys two primary meanings. The first is an imprecise sense of harmonious or aesthetically-pleasing proportionality and balance; such that it reflects beauty or perfection. The second meaning is a precise and well-defined concept of balance or 'patterned self-similarity' that can be demonstrated or proved according to the rules of a formal system: by geometry, through physics or otherwise.
a. Tessellation
b. Symmetry breaking
c. Molecular symmetry
d. Symmetry

45. In optics, _____ is the phenomenon in which the phase velocity of a wave depends on its frequency. Media having such a property are termed dispersive media.

The most familiar example of _____ is probably a rainbow, in which _____ causes the spatial separation of a white light into components of different wavelengths.

   a. Crib
   c. Depth
   b. Dispersion
   d. Boussinesq approximation

46. In descriptive statistics, the _____ is the length of the smallest interval which contains all the data. It is calculated by subtracting the smallest observations from the greatest and provides an indication of statistical dispersion.

It is measured in the same units as the data.

   a. Range
   c. Kernel
   b. Class
   d. Bandwidth

47. In mathematics and statistics, _____ is a measure of difference for interval and ratio variables between the observed value and the mean. The sign of _____, either positive or negative, indicates whether the observation is larger than or smaller than the mean. The magnitude of the value reports how different an observation is from the mean.

   a. Filter
   c. Functional
   b. Conchoid
   d. Deviation

48. In probability and statistics, the _____ is a measure of the dispersion of a collection of numbers. It can apply to a probability distribution, a random variable, a population or a data set. The _____ is usually denoted with the letter σ.

   a. Failure rate
   c. Statistical population
   b. Standard deviation
   d. Null hypothesis

49. In probability theory and statistics, the _____ of a random variable, probability distribution averaging the squared distance of its possible values from the expected value. Whereas the mean is a way to describe the location of a distribution, the _____ is a way to capture its scale or degree of being spread out. The unit of _____ is the square of the unit of the original variable.

   a. Kendall tau rank correlation coefficient
   c. Nonlinear regression
   b. Variance
   d. Probability distribution

50. _____ (May 16 [O.S. May 4] 1821 - December 8 [O.S. November 26] 1894) was a Russian mathematician. His name can be alternatively transliterated as Chebychev, Chebyshov, Tchebycheff or Tschebyscheff .

One of nine children, Chebyshev was born in the village of Okatovo in the district of Borovsk, province of Kaluga.

   a. Girard Desargues
   c. Pafnuty Lvovich Chebyshev
   b. Fibonacci
   d. Serre

51. In mathematics, the _____ of a non-negative integer n, denoted by n!, is the product of all positive integers less than or equal to n. For example,

$$5! = 1 \times 2 \times 3 \times 4 \times 5 = 120$$

and

$$6! = 1 \times 2 \times 3 \times 4 \times 5 \times 6 = 720$$

The notation n! was introduced by Christian Kramp in 1808.

The _____ function is formally defined by

$$n! = \prod_{k=1}^{n} k \qquad \forall n \in \mathbb{N}.$$

The above definition incorporates the instance

$$0! = 1$$

as an instance of the fact that the product of no numbers at all is 1.

- a. Plane partition
- b. Factorial
- c. Partition of a set
- d. Symbolic combinatorics

52. _____ is a dimensionless quantity derived by subtracting the population mean from an individual raw score and then dividing the difference by the population standard deviation.
- a. 2-3 heap
- b. 120-cell
- c. 1-center problem
- d. Z-score

53. A _____ is the value of a variable below which a certain percent of observations fall. So the 20th _____ is the value below which 20 percent of the observations may be found. The term _____ and the related term _____ rank are often used in descriptive statistics as well as in the reporting of scores from norm-referenced tests.
- a. Percentile
- b. Frequency distribution
- c. Logistic regression
- d. Statistically significant

54. In descriptive statistics, a _____ is any of the three values which divide the sorted data set into four equal parts, so that each part represents one fourth of the sampled population.

- first _____ = lower _____ = cuts off lowest 25% of data = 25th percentile
- second _____ = median = cuts data set in half = 50th percentile
- third _____ = upper _____ = cuts off highest 25% of data, or lowest 75% = 75th percentile

The difference between the upper and lower _____s is called the interquartile range.

There is no universal agreement on choosing the _____ values.

Chapter 13. Statistics

The formula for the position of the observation at a given percentile, y, with n data points sorted in ascending order is:

$$L_y = (n+1)(\frac{y}{100})$$

Example 4.
- a. Trimean
- b. Mean reciprocal rank
- c. Quartile
- d. Seven-number summary

55. In descriptive statistics, the _____ middle fifty and middle of the #s, is a measure of statistical dispersion, being equal to the difference between the third and first quartiles.

Unlike the range, the _____ is a robust statistic, having a breakdown point of 25%, and is thus often preferred to the total range.

The IQR is used to build box plots, simple graphical representations of a probability distribution.

- a. Interquartile range
- b. Unitized risk
- c. A chemical equation
- d. A Mathematical Theory of Communication

56. In statistics, the mid-range or mid-extreme of a set of statistical data values is the arithmetic mean of the maximum and minimum values in a data set, or:

$$\frac{\max x + \min x}{2}.$$

As such it is a measure of central tendency.

The _____ is highly sensitive to outliers and ignores all but two data points. It is therefore a very non-robust statistic, and it is rarely used in statistical analysis.

- a. Geometric-harmonic mean
- b. Weighted mean
- c. Mean of circular quantities
- d. Midrange

57. In mathematics, a _____ is a constant multiplicative factor of a certain object. For example, in the expression $9x^2$, the _____ of x^2 is 9.

The object can be such things as a variable, a vector, a function, etc.

- a. Coefficient
- b. Fibonacci polynomials
- c. Stability radius
- d. Multivariate division algorithm

58. In probability theory, a probability distribution is called discrete if it is characterized by a probability mass function. Thus, the distribution of a random variable X is discrete, and X is then called a _____, if

$$\sum_u \Pr(X = u) = 1$$

as u runs through the set of all possible values of X.

If a random variable is discrete, then the set of all values that it can assume with non-zero probability is finite or countably infinite, because the sum of uncountably many positive real numbers always diverges to infinity.

a. Statistics
b. Regression toward the mean
c. First-hitting-time models
d. Discrete random variable

59. In probability theory and statistics, a _____ identifies either the probability of each value of an unidentified random variable, or the probability of the value falling within a particular interval. The probability function describes the range of possible values that a random variable can attain and the probability that the value of the random variable is within any subset of that range.

When the random variable takes values in the set of real numbers, the _____ is completely described by the cumulative distribution function, whose value at each real x is the probability that the random variable is smaller than or equal to x.

a. Statistical graphics
b. Probability distribution
c. Normal distribution
d. Z-test

60. In mathematics, _____ are used in the study of chance and probability. They were developed to assist in the analysis of games of chance, stochastic events, and the results of scientific experiments by capturing only the mathematical properties necessary to answer probabilistic questions. Further formalizations have firmly grounded the entity in the theoretical domains of mathematics by making use of measure theory.

a. Statistical dispersion
b. Median polish
c. Statistics
d. Random variables

61. In probability theory, a probability distribution is called _____ if its cumulative distribution function is _____. That is equivalent to saying that for random variables X with the distribution in question, Pr[X = a] = 0 for all real numbers a. If the distribution of X is _____ then X is called a _____ random variable.

a. Continuous phase modulation
b. Concatenated codes
c. Continuous
d. Conull set

62. In mathematics, specifically in combinatorial commutative algebra, a convex lattice polytope P is called _____ if it has the following property: given any positive integer n, every lattice point of the dilation nP, obtained from P by scaling its vertices by the factor n and taking the convex hull of the resulting points, can be written as the sum of exactly n lattice points in P. This property plays an important role in the theory of toric varieties, where it corresponds to projective normality of the toric variety determined by P.

The simplex in R^k with the vertices at the origin and along the unit coordinate vectors is _____.

a. Polytetrahedron
b. Hypercube
c. Normal
d. Demihypercubes

63. The _____ is an important family of continuous probability distributions, applicable in many fields. Each member of the family may be defined by two parameters, location and scale: the mean and variance respectively. The standard _____ is the _____ with a mean of zero and a variance of one.

a. Normal Distribution
b. Null hypothesis
c. Percentile rank
d. Coefficient of variation

64. _____ Galilei (15 February 1564 - 8 January 1642) was a Tuscan physicist, mathematician, astronomer, and philosopher who played a major role in the Scientific Revolution. His achievements include improvements to the telescope and consequent astronomical observations, and support for Copernicanism. _____ has been called the 'father of modern observational astronomy', the 'father of modern physics', the 'father of science', and 'the Father of Modern Science.' The motion of uniformly accelerated objects, taught in nearly all high school and introductory college physics courses, was studied by _____ as the subject of kinematics.

a. Jan Kowalewski
b. David Naccache
c. Francesco Severi
d. Galileo

65. In mathematics, the concept of a _____ tries to capture the intuitive idea of a geometrical one-dimensional and continuous object. A simple example is the circle. In everyday use of the term '_____', a straight line is not curved, but in mathematical parlance _____s include straight lines and line segments.

a. Negative pedal curve
b. Quadrifolium
c. Kappa curve
d. Curve

66. An _____ of a real-valued function y = f(x) is a curve which describes the behavior of f as either x or y tends to infinity.

In other words, as one moves along the graph of f(x) in some direction, the distance between it and the _____ eventually becomes smaller than any distance that one may specify.

If a curve A has the curve B as an _____, one says that A is asymptotic to B. Similarly B is asymptotic to A, so A and B are called asymptotic.

a. Improper integral
b. Asymptote
c. Isoperimetric dimension
d. Infinite product

67. In statistics, _____ is a collective name for techniques for the modeling and analysis of numerical data consisting of values of a dependent variable and of one or more independent variables. The dependent variable in the regression equation is modeled as a function of the independent variables, corresponding parameters, and an error term. The error term is treated as a random variable.

a. 1-center problem
b. 2-3 heap
c. 120-cell
d. Regression analysis

Chapter 13. Statistics

68. The method of _____ or ordinary _____ is used to solve overdetermined systems. _____ is often applied in statistical contexts, particularly regression analysis.

_____ can be interpreted as a method of fitting data.

a. Non-linear least squares
c. Least squares
b. Rata Die
d. System equivalence

69. In mathematics and in the sciences, a _____ (plural: _____e, formulæ or _____s) is a concise way of expressing information symbolically (as in a mathematical or chemical _____), or a general relationship between quantities. One of many famous _____e is Albert Einstein's $E = mc^2$ (see special relativity

In mathematics, a _____ is a key to solve an equation with variables. For example, the problem of determining the volume of a sphere is one that requires a significant amount of integral calculus to solve.

a. 1-center problem
c. 120-cell
b. 2-3 heap
d. Formula

Chapter 14. Consumer Mathematics

1. _____ is a fee, paid on borrowed capital. Assets lent include money, shares, consumer goods through hire purchase, major assets such as aircraft, and even entire factories in finance lease arrangements. The _____ is calculated upon the value of the assets in the same manner as upon money.

 a. Interest
 b. Interest expense
 c. Interest sensitivity gap
 d. A Mathematical Theory of Communication

2. _____ is the concept of adding accumulated interest back to the principal, so that interest is earned on interest from that moment on. The act of declaring interest to be principal is called compounding. A loan, for example, may have its interest compounded every month: in this case, a loan with $100 principal and 1% interest per month would have a balance of $101 at the end of the first month.

 a. Net interest margin securities
 b. Net interest margin
 c. Retained interest
 d. Compound Interest

3. In computational complexity theory, an algorithm is said to take _____ if the asymptotic upper bound for the time it requires is proportional to the size of the input, which is usually denoted n.

Informally spoken, the running time increases linearly with the size of the input. For example, a procedure that adds up all elements of a list requires time proportional to the length of the list.

 a. Linear time
 b. Constructible function
 c. Truth table reduction
 d. Time-constructible function

4. In abstract algebra, a module S over a ring R is called _____ or irreducible if it is not the zero module 0 and if its only submodules are 0 and S. Understanding the _____ modules over a ring is usually helpful because these modules form the 'building blocks' of all other modules in a certain sense.

Abelian groups are the same as Z-modules.

 a. Harmonic series
 b. Basis
 c. Simple
 d. Derivation

5. A _____ typically refers to a class of handheld calculators that are capable of plotting graphs, solving simultaneous equations, and performing numerous other tasks with variables. Most popular _____s are also programmable, allowing the user to create customized programs, typically for scientific/engineering and education applications. Due to their large displays intended for graphing, they can also accommodate several lines of text and calculations at a time.

 a. Graphing calculator
 b. Support vector machines
 c. Genus
 d. Bump mapping

6. A _____ is a device for performing mathematical calculations, distinguished from a computer by having a limited problem solving ability and an interface optimized for interactive calculation rather than programming. _____s can be hardware or software, and mechanical or electronic, and are often built into devices such as PDAs or mobile phones.

Modern electronic _____s are generally small, digital, and usually inexpensive.

 a. 1-center problem
 b. 120-cell
 c. 2-3 heap
 d. Calculator

Chapter 14. Consumer Mathematics

7. In mathematics, the _____ of a number to a given base is the power or exponent to which the base must be raised in order to produce the number.

For example, the _____ of 1000 to the base 10 is 3, because 3 is how many 10s one must multiply to get 1000: thus 10 × 10 × 10 = 1000; the base-2 _____ of 32 is 5 because 5 is how many 2s one must multiply to get 32: thus 2 × 2 × 2 × 2 × 2 = 32. In the language of exponents: 10^3 = 1000, so $\log_{10} 1000 = 3$, and $2^5 = 32$, so $\log_2 32 = 5$.

 a. 2-3 heap
 b. Logarithm
 c. 1-center problem
 d. 120-cell

8. In mathematics, a _____ is a number that can be expressed as an integral of an algebraic function over an algebraic domain. Kontsevich and Zagier define a _____ as a complex number whose real and imaginary parts are values of absolutely convergent integrals of rational functions with rational coefficients, over domains in given by polynomial inequalities with rational coefficients.

 a. Closeness
 b. Boussinesq approximation
 c. Disk
 d. Period

9. _____ is a legal term (in some jurisdictions, notably in the USA, United Kingdom, Canada, and Australia) that encompasses land along with anything permanently affixed to the land, such as buildings, specifically property that is stationary, or fixed in location. _____ law is the body of regulations and legal codes which pertain to such matters under a particular jurisdiction. _____ is often considered synonymous with real property (also sometimes called realty), in contrast with personal property (also sometimes called chattel or personalty under chattel law or personal property law.)

 a. 1-center problem
 b. 120-cell
 c. Home equity
 d. Real estate

10. In mathematics, an _____, or central tendency of a data set refers to a measure of the 'middle' or 'expected' value of the data set. There are many different descriptive statistics that can be chosen as a measurement of the central tendency of the data items.

An _____ is a single value that is meant to typify a list of values.

 a. A chemical equation
 b. Average
 c. A posteriori
 d. A Mathematical Theory of Communication

11. A _____ is the transfer of an interest in property (or in law the equivalent - a charge) to a lender as a security for a debt - usually a loan of money. While a _____ in itself is not a debt, it is lender's security for a debt. It is a transfer of an interest in land (or the equivalent), from the owner to the _____ lender, on the condition that this interest will be returned to the owner of the real estate when the terms of the _____ have been satisfied or performed.

 a. 1-center problem
 b. 120-cell
 c. 2-3 heap
 d. Mortgage

12. The terms _____, nominal APR, and effective APR describe the interest rate for a whole year, rather than just a monthly fee/rate, as applied on a loan, mortgage, credit card, etc. Those terms have formal, legal definitions in some countries or legal jurisdictions, but in general:

- The nominal APR is the simple-interest rate.
- The effective APR is the fee+compound interest rate.

The nominal APR is calculated as: the rate, for a payment period, multiplied by the number of payment periods in a year. However, the exact legal definition of 'effective APR' can vary greatly in each jurisdiction, depending on the type of fees included, such as participation fees, loan origination fees, monthly service charges, or late fees. The effective APR has been called the 'mathematically-true' interest rate for each year. The computation for the effective APR, as the fee+compound interest rate, can also vary depending on whether the up-front fees, such as origination or participation fees, are added to the entire amount, or treated as a short-term loan due in the first payment.

a. Annual percentage rate
b. A posteriori
c. A Mathematical Theory of Communication
d. A chemical equation

13. In mathematics, a _____ is a way of expressing a number as a fraction of 100. It is often denoted using the percent sign, '%'. For example, 45% is equal to 45 / 100, or 0.45.

a. Percentage
b. Subtrahend
c. Lowest common denominator
d. Least common multiple

14. _____ or amortisation is the process of decreasing an amount over a period of time. The word comes from Middle English amortisen to kill, alienate in mortmain, from Anglo-French amorteser, alteration of amortir, from Vulgar Latin admortire to kill, from Latin ad- + mort-, mors death. Particular instances of the term include:

- _____, the allocation of a lump sum amount to different time periods, particularly for loans and other forms of finance, including related interest or other finance charges.
    - _____ schedule, a table detailing each periodic payment on a loan, as generated by an _____ calculator.
    - Negative _____, an _____ schedule where the loan amount actually increases through not paying the full interest
- Amortized analysis, analyzing the execution cost of algorithms over a sequence of operations.
- _____ of capital expenditures of certain assets under accounting rules, particularly intangible assets, in a manner analogous to depreciation.
- _____

_____ is also used in the context of zoning regulations and describes the time in which a property owner has to relocate when the property's use constitutes a preexisting nonconforming use under zoning regulations.

- Depreciation

a. ISAAC
b. Amortization
c. Origin
d. Identity

Chapter 14. Consumer Mathematics

15. In mathematics and in the sciences, a _____ (plural: _____e, formulæ or _____s) is a concise way of expressing information symbolically (as in a mathematical or chemical _____), or a general relationship between quantities. One of many famous _____e is Albert Einstein's E = mc² (see special relativity

In mathematics, a _____ is a key to solve an equation with variables. For example, the problem of determining the volume of a sphere is one that requires a significant amount of integral calculus to solve.

   a. Formula
   c. 120-cell
   b. 1-center problem
   d. 2-3 heap

16. _____s are payments made by a corporation to its shareholder members. When a corporation earns a profit or surplus, that money can be put to two uses: it can either be re-invested in the business, or it can be paid to the shareholders as a _____. Many corporations retain a portion of their earnings and pay the remainder as a _____.

   a. Dividend
   c. GNU Privacy Guard
   b. 120-cell
   d. 1-center problem

17. In finance, _____ rate of profit or sometimes just return, is the ratio of money gained or lost on an investment relative to the amount of money invested. The amount of money gained or lost may be referred to as interest, profit/loss, gain/loss, or net income/loss. The money invested may be referred to as the asset, capital, principal, or the cost basis of the investment.

   a. 1-center problem
   c. Return on equity
   b. P/E ratio
   d. Rate of return

18. A _____ is a party that mediates between a buyer and a seller. A _____ who also acts as a seller or as a buyer becomes a principal party to the deal. Distinguish agent: one who acts on behalf of a principal.

   a. 120-cell
   c. 2-3 heap
   b. 1-center problem
   d. Broker

19. In mathematics, the concept of a '_____' is used to describe the behavior of a function as its argument or input either 'gets close' to some point, or as the argument becomes arbitrarily large; or the behavior of a sequence's elements as their index increases indefinitely. _____s are used in calculus and other branches of mathematical analysis to define derivatives and continuity.

In formulas, _____ is usually abbreviated as lim.

   a. Duality
   c. Copula
   b. Contact
   d. Limit

20. Suppose that φ : M → N is a smooth map between smooth manifolds; then the _____ of φ at a point x is, in some sense, the best linear approximation of φ near x. It can be viewed as generalization of the total derivative of ordinary calculus. Explicitly, it is a linear map from the tangent space of M at x to the tangent space of N at φ

   a. Boundary
   c. Concurrent
   b. Differential
   d. Grill

Chapter 14. Consumer Mathematics

21. In mathematics, an _____ in the sense of ring theory is a subring $\mathcal{O}$ of a ring R that satisfies the conditions

   1. R is a ring which is a finite-dimensional algebra over the rational number field $\mathbb{Q}$
   2. $\mathcal{O}$ spans R over $\mathbb{Q}$, so that $\mathbb{Q}\mathcal{O} = R$, and
   3. $\mathcal{O}$ is a lattice in R.

The third condition can be stated more accurately, in terms of the extension of scalars of R to the real numbers, embedding R in a real vector space. In less formal terms, additively $\mathcal{O}$ should be a free abelian group generated by a basis for R over $\mathbb{Q}$.

The leading example is the case where R is a number field K and $\mathcal{O}$ is its ring of integers. In algebraic number theory there are examples for any K other than the rational field of proper subrings of the ring of integers that are also _____s.

   a. Algebraic
   c. Annihilator
   b. Efficiency
   d. Order

22. The term _____ refers to the central sense organ complex, for those animals that have one, normally on the ventral surface of the head and can depending on the definition in the human case, include the hair, forehead, eyebrow, eyes, nose, ears, cheeks, mouth, lips, philtrum, teeth, skin, and chin. The _____ has uses of expression, appearance, and identity amongst others.It also has different senses like smelling, tasting, hearing, and seeing.

Caricatures often exaggerate facial features to make a _____ more easily recognized in association with a pronounced portion of the _____ of the individual in question--for example, a caricature of Osama bin Laden might focus on his facial hair and nose; a caricature of George W. Bush might enlarge his ears to the size of an elephant¢s; a caricature of Jay Leno may pronounce his head and chin; and a caricature of Mick Jagger might enlarge his lips.

   a. 120-cell
   c. Face
   b. 2-3 heap
   d. 1-center problem

23. In set theory and its applications throughout mathematics, a _____ is a collection of sets that can be unambiguously defined by a property that all its members share. The precise definition of '_____' depends on foundational context. In work on ZF set theory, the notion of _____ is informal, whereas other set theories, such as NBG set theory, axiomatize the notion of '_____'.

   a. Congruent
   c. Class
   b. Filter
   d. Coherence

24. In graph theory, an _____ is a path in a graph which visits each edge exactly once. Similarly, an Eulerian circuit is an _____ which starts and ends on the same vertex. They were first discussed by Leonhard Euler while solving the famous Seven Bridges of Königsberg problem in 1736.

   a. Isomorphism of graphs
   c. Eulerian path
   b. Adjacent vertex
   d. Independent set

25. In mathematics and computer science, _____ is the study of graphs: mathematical structures used to model pairwise relations between objects from a certain collection. A 'graph' in this context refers to a collection of vertices or 'nodes' and a collection of edges that connect pairs of vertices. A graph may be undirected, meaning that there is no distinction between the two vertices associated with each edge, or its edges may be directed from one vertex to another; see graph for more detailed definitions and for other variations in the types of graphs that are commonly considered.
   a. Pooling design
   b. Partial equivalence relation
   c. Discrete mathematics
   d. Graph theory

26. The word _____ has many distinct meanings in different fields of knowledge, depending on their methodologies and the context of discussion. Broadly speaking we can say that a _____ is some kind of belief or claim that (supposedly) explains, asserts, or consolidates some class of claims. Additionally, in contrast with a theorem the statement of the _____ is generally accepted only in some tentative fashion as opposed to regarding it as having been conclusively established.
   a. Per mil
   b. Transport of structure
   c. Defined
   d. Theory

27. In geometry, a _____ is a special kind of point, usually a corner of a polygon, polyhedron, or higher dimensional polytope. In the geometry of curves a _____ is a point of where the first derivative of curvature is zero. In graph theory, a _____ is the fundamental unit out of which graphs are formed
   a. Vertex
   b. Crib
   c. Duality
   d. Dini

28. In geometry and trigonometry, an _____ is the figure formed by two rays sharing a common endpoint, called the vertex of the _____. The magnitude of the _____ is the 'amount of rotation' that separates the two rays, and can be measured by considering the length of circular arc swept out when one ray is rotated about the vertex to coincide with the other. Where there is no possibility of confusion, the term '_____' is used interchangeably for both the geometric configuration itself and for its angular magnitude.
   a. A Mathematical Theory of Communication
   b. A chemical equation
   c. A posteriori
   d. Angle

29. In mathematics, the _____ of a Euclidean space is a special point, usually denoted by the letter O, used as a fixed point of reference for the geometry of the surrounding space. In a Cartesian coordinate system, the _____ is the point where the axes of the system intersect. In Euclidean geometry, the _____ may be chosen freely as any convenient point of reference.
   a. Origin
   b. Interval
   c. Autonomous system
   d. OMAC

30. In graph theory, a _____ in a graph is a sequence of vertices such that from each of its vertices there is an edge to the next vertex in the sequence. The first vertex is called the start vertex and the last vertex is called the end vertex. Both of them are called end or terminal vertices of the _____.
   a. Class
   b. Blinding
   c. Path
   d. Deltoid

156   Chapter 14. Consumer Mathematics

31. In category theory, two categories C and D are _____ if there exist functors F : C → D and G : D → C which are mutually inverse to each other. This means that both the objects and the morphisms of C and D stand in a one to one correspondence to each other. Two _____ categories share all properties that are defined solely in terms of category theory; for all practical purposes, they are identical and differ only in the notation of their objects and morphisms.
   a. Automorphism group
   c. Epimorphism
   b. Isomorphism
   d. Isomorphic

32. In mathematics, a _____ is a statement that can be proved on the basis of explicitly stated or previously agreed assumptions.
   a. Boolean function
   c. Disjunction introduction
   b. Theorem
   d. Logical value

33. Walking is the main form of animal locomotion on land, distinguished from running and crawling. When carried out in shallow waters, it is usually described as wading and when performed over a steeply rising object or an obstacle it becomes scrambling or climbing. The word _____ is descended from the Old English wealcan 'to roll'.
   a. 2-3 heap
   c. Walk
   b. 1-center problem
   d. 120-cell

34. A _____ is a complex tour puzzle in the form of a complex branching passage through which the solver must find a route. This is different from a labyrinth, which has an actual through-route and is not designed to be difficult to navigate. The pathways and walls in a _____ or labyrinth are fixed.
   a. 2-3 heap
   c. Maze
   b. 120-cell
   d. 1-center problem

35. In the physical sciences, _____ is a measurement of the gravitational force acting on an object. Near the surface of the Earth, the acceleration due to gravity is approximately constant; this means that an object's _____ is roughly proportional to its mass.

In commerce and in many other applications, _____ means the same as mass as that term is used in physics.

   a. 120-cell
   c. 1-center problem
   b. Weight
   d. 2-3 heap

36. In mathematical analysis, a metric space M is said to be _____ (or Cauchy) if every Cauchy sequence of points in M has a limit that is also in M or alternatively if every Cauchy sequence in M converges in M.

Intuitively, a space is _____ if there are no 'points missing' from it (inside or at the boundary.) For instance, the set of rational numbers is not _____, because $\sqrt{2}$ is 'missing' from it, even though one can construct a Cauchy sequence of rational numbers that converges to it.

   a. Complete
   c. 1-center problem
   b. 2-3 heap
   d. 120-cell

37. In the mathematical field of graph theory, a _____ is a simple graph in which every pair of distinct vertices is connected by an edge. The _____ on n vertices has n vertices and n edges, and is denoted by K_n. It is a regular graph of degree n − 1.

Chapter 14. Consumer Mathematics

a. 1-center problem
b. Wheel graph
c. 120-cell
d. Complete Graph

38. A _____ is a structure built to span a gorge, valley, road, railroad track, river, body of water for the purpose of providing passage over the obstacle. Designs of _____s will vary depending on the function of the _____ and the nature of the terrain where the _____ is to be constructed. Roman _____ of Córdoba, Spain, built in the 1st century BC. Ponte di Pietra in Verona, Italy. A log _____ in the French Alps near Vallorcine. An English 18th century example of a _____ in the Palladian style, with shops on the span: Pulteney _____, Bath A Han Dynasty Chinese miniature model of two residential towers joined by a _____

The first _____s were made by nature -- as simple as a log fallen across a stream.

a. 1-center problem
b. 2-3 heap
c. 120-cell
d. Bridge

39. In mathematics, computing, linguistics and related subjects, an _____ is a sequence of finite instructions, often used for calculation and data processing. It is formally a type of effective method in which a list of well-defined instructions for completing a task will, when given an initial state, proceed through a well-defined series of successive states, eventually terminating in an end-state. The transition from one state to the next is not necessarily deterministic; some _____s, known as probabilistic _____s, incorporate randomness.

a. In-place algorithm
b. Out-of-core
c. Approximate counting algorithm
d. Algorithm

40. The _____ program is a directory search utility on Unix-like platforms. It searches through one or more directory trees of a filesystem, locating files based on some user-specified criteria. By default, _____ returns all files below the current working directory.

a. 1-center problem
b. Find
c. 120-cell
d. 2-3 heap

41. Wikipedia has thousands of topic lists; some are even lists of other lists

_____ - By belief - By nationality - By occupation - By office held - By prize won

a. William Hugh Woodin
b. George Glauberman
c. People
d. Kenneth Kunen

42. A _____ is a structured activity, usually undertaken for enjoyment and sometimes also used as an educational tool. _____s are distinct from work, which is usually carried out for remuneration, and from art, which is more concerned with the expression of ideas. However, the distinction is not clear-cut, and many _____s are also considered to be work (such as professional players of spectator sports/_____s) or art (such as jigsaw puzzles or _____s involving an artistic layout such as Mah-jongg solitaire.)

a. 2-3 heap
b. 1-center problem
c. 120-cell
d. Game

43. _____ is a book by Matt Curtin about cryptography.

In this book, the author accounts his involvement in the DESCHALL Project, mobilizing thousands of personal computers in 1997 in order to meet the challenge to crack a single message encrypted with DES.

This was and remains one of the largest collaborations of any kind on a single project in history.

a. Development
b. Congruent
c. Brute force
d. Blind

44. The _____ in operations research is a problem in discrete or combinatorial optimization. It is a prominent illustration of a class of problems in computational complexity theory which are classified as NP-hard.

The problem is: given a number of cities and the costs of travelling from any city to any other city, what is the least-cost round-trip route that visits each city exactly once and then returns to the starting city?

Given a number of cities and the costs of travelling from any city to any other city, what is the least-cost round-trip route that visits each city exactly once and then returns to the starting city?

The size of the solution space is!/2 for n > 2, where n is the number of cities.

a. New digraph reconstruction conjecture
b. Cut vertex
c. Snake-in-the-box
d. Travelling salesman problem

ANSWER KEY

Chapter 1
1. c   2. b   3. b   4. d   5. b   6. c   7. b   8. c   9. d   10. d
11. d   12. c   13. d   14. b   15. d   16. d   17. d   18. d   19. d   20. a
21. a   22. d   23. d   24. d   25. c   26. d   27. d   28. a   29. d   30. a
31. b   32. d   33. c   34. b   35. d   36. d   37. d   38. d   39. c   40. d
41. d   42. c   43. d   44. d

Chapter 2
1. a   2. d   3. a   4. c   5. b   6. d   7. d   8. b   9. a   10. a
11. a   12. d   13. d   14. b   15. d   16. b   17. a   18. a   19. b   20. a
21. a   22. c   23. a   24. a   25. c   26. b   27. d   28. c   29. d   30. d
31. b   32. d   33. c   34. d   35. b   36. c   37. b   38. d   39. b   40. c
41. a   42. b   43. d   44. c

Chapter 3
1. d   2. d   3. a   4. a   5. d   6. c   7. a   8. d   9. c   10. d
11. d   12. d   13. d   14. d   15. a   16. d   17. d   18. d   19. c   20. d
21. a

Chapter 4
1. d   2. d   3. d   4. d   5. d   6. d   7. d   8. d   9. c   10. c
11. d   12. d   13. d   14. a   15. d   16. d   17. b   18. d   19. d   20. b
21. b   22. a   23. c   24. b   25. b   26. b   27. d   28. c   29. d   30. c
31. a   32. b   33. d   34. c   35. d   36. b   37. d   38. d

Chapter 5
1. d   2. d   3. a   4. d   5. d   6. d   7. d   8. d   9. a   10. b
11. b   12. d   13. d   14. b   15. b   16. d   17. a   18. c   19. d   20. b
21. d   22. d   23. b   24. a   25. d   26. b   27. d   28. b   29. a   30. a
31. c   32. d   33. c   34. d   35. d   36. d   37. b   38. d   39. d   40. c
41. d   42. d   43. a   44. c   45. a   46. d   47. d   48. d   49. b   50. c
51. d   52. b   53. d   54. d   55. d   56. b   57. c   58. d   59. b

Chapter 6
1. c   2. d   3. d   4. d   5. c   6. d   7. d   8. a   9. d   10. d
11. a   12. d   13. c   14. a   15. c   16. b   17. d   18. b   19. d   20. a
21. c   22. d   23. a   24. b   25. a   26. b   27. d   28. d   29. d   30. d
31. c   32. a   33. b   34. d   35. a   36. d   37. d   38. c   39. b   40. c
41. d   42. a   43. d   44. d   45. d   46. a   47. d   48. d   49. a   50. c
51. a   52. c   53. d   54. c   55. d   56. d

Chapter 7

1. d	2. d	3. c	4. b	5. a	6. c	7. d	8. d	9. b	10. c
11. b	12. d	13. d	14. b	15. a	16. c	17. c	18. b	19. d	20. a
21. d	22. d	23. b	24. d	25. d	26. d	27. c	28. a	29. c	30. d
31. d	32. a	33. a	34. d	35. a	36. a	37. a	38. a	39. b	40. a
41. a	42. a	43. a	44. d	45. d	46. b	47. d	48. a	49. c	50. d
51. d	52. c	53. d	54. d	55. c	56. d	57. d			

Chapter 8

1. d	2. d	3. c	4. a	5. c	6. d	7. d	8. d	9. d	10. d
11. d	12. d	13. a	14. d	15. a	16. d	17. c	18. a	19. d	20. c
21. d	22. d	23. d	24. d	25. a	26. a	27. d	28. b	29. a	30. c
31. d	32. d	33. c	34. b	35. d	36. c	37. d	38. c	39. d	40. d
41. d	42. b	43. d	44. a	45. d	46. a	47. d	48. c	49. b	50. a
51. d	52. d	53. c	54. d	55. d	56. d	57. d	58. a	59. b	60. d
61. d	62. a	63. d	64. d	65. d					

Chapter 9

1. d	2. d	3. d	4. a	5. d	6. b	7. d	8. d	9. d	10. d
11. c	12. d	13. d	14. b	15. a	16. d	17. a	18. d	19. d	20. c
21. b	22. b	23. d	24. d	25. d	26. d	27. d	28. d	29. d	30. d
31. d	32. d	33. c	34. b	35. c	36. d	37. b	38. a	39. b	40. d
41. a	42. d	43. c	44. d	45. b	46. c	47. d	48. d	49. d	50. d
51. d	52. d	53. d	54. d	55. b	56. d	57. d	58. a	59. d	60. d
61. b	62. c	63. d	64. d	65. d	66. b	67. d	68. d	69. d	70. b
71. a	72. d	73. c	74. d	75. d	76. b	77. c	78. d	79. c	80. d
81. d	82. c	83. c	84. d	85. d	86. a	87. c	88. d	89. d	90. d
91. a	92. b	93. d	94. d	95. b	96. b	97. d	98. d	99. b	100. d
101. b	102. a	103. b							

Chapter 10

1. d	2. a	3. b	4. d	5. d	6. d	7. d	8. d	9. d	10. b
11. c	12. b	13. a	14. b	15. d	16. b	17. d	18. c	19. d	20. b
21. c	22. a	23. c	24. d	25. c	26. d	27. a	28. d	29. c	30. d
31. b	32. a	33. d	34. c	35. b	36. a	37. d	38. b	39. d	40. d
41. b	42. b	43. b	44. d	45. c					

Chapter 11

1. d	2. c	3. d	4. b	5. d	6. a	7. d	8. d	9. d	10. d
11. b	12. d	13. b	14. d	15. d	16. d	17. c			

ANSWER KEY

Chapter 12

1. d	2. b	3. c	4. d	5. d	6. a	7. d	8. d	9. d	10. d
11. b	12. a	13. c	14. d	15. a	16. a	17. a	18. d	19. d	20. b
21. c	22. a	23. d	24. b	25. b	26. d	27. a	28. d	29. d	30. a
31. c	32. d	33. d	34. c	35. b	36. d	37. d			

Chapter 13

1. c	2. b	3. d	4. a	5. d	6. c	7. b	8. b	9. d	10. a
11. a	12. b	13. d	14. c	15. a	16. b	17. d	18. d	19. d	20. d
21. a	22. b	23. c	24. d	25. b	26. c	27. b	28. a	29. d	30. b
31. b	32. b	33. b	34. d	35. a	36. a	37. d	38. d	39. a	40. b
41. a	42. c	43. c	44. d	45. b	46. a	47. d	48. b	49. b	50. c
51. b	52. d	53. a	54. c	55. a	56. d	57. a	58. d	59. b	60. d
61. c	62. c	63. a	64. d	65. d	66. b	67. d	68. c	69. d	

Chapter 14

1. a	2. d	3. a	4. c	5. a	6. d	7. b	8. d	9. d	10. b
11. d	12. a	13. a	14. b	15. a	16. a	17. d	18. d	19. d	20. b
21. d	22. c	23. c	24. c	25. d	26. d	27. a	28. d	29. a	30. c
31. d	32. b	33. c	34. c	35. b	36. a	37. d	38. d	39. d	40. b
41. c	42. d	43. c	44. d